THE
CHRISTIAN
IN
AN
AGE
OF
SEXUAL
ECLIPSE

MICHAEL
BRAUN
&
GEORGE
ALAN
REKERS PhD

 Tyndale House
Publishers, Inc.
Wheaton, Illinois

Library of Congress Catalog
Card Number 81-50142
ISBN 0-8423-0256-5, paper
Copyright © 1981 by
Michael Braun and George
A. Rekers. All rights
reserved.

First printing, May 1981.
Printed in the United States
of America.

Scripture quotations are
from the Revised Standard
Version unless otherwise
indicated.

For Susan and for Sharon
UXORIBUS NOSTRIS
Quarum Amore Amorem Dei Vidimus

CONTENTS

ACKNOWLEDGMENTS

We wish to express a deep sense of gratitude to the many who encouraged and assisted us in the production of this work. As one might expect, it is impossible to recognize everyone who played an important part in the thoughts as well as the words that appear on these pages. Nevertheless, some debts of gratitude must be acknowledged: Our first debt is to our wives, whose constant support and occasional admonitions took us "to school" in the matter of godly and biblical patterns of behavior within marriage and the family. We lovingly dedicate this book to Susan and Sharon.

Next in line stand our children: Mike, Jr., Robin (who used to be called "Bunny"), Erik, Adam, and Kristen Braun; and Steven, Andrew, and Matthew Rekers. We were able to write these words with their permission—the permission that faithful, obedient, and loving children give their fathers who would desire to be elders in the church.

To all the saints at Community Evangelical Free Church in Gainesville, Florida, we wish to acknowledge a special debt of gratitude. Their fellowship made this work possible.

Several individuals read the entire manuscript and offered invaluable comments. Our thanks go to Dr. Judy Sanders, whose keen eye, ready mind, and nimble typing fingers played an inestimable part in this work. To Miss Carol Brown, soon to be Dr. Brown, we owe a special word of thanks. And to Dr. Gary Miller, who respectfully disagreed with almost everything within these pages, yet kindly read them and convinced us further that we were, in part at least, hitting the mark, we are especially grateful.

Dr. Reed Bell and his wife Nell gave us a great deal of help in compiling information on the radical feminist movement. We are grateful for their invaluable assistance.

Others read and made comments on various portions of the book. Our warmest thanks go to Dr. John Sommerville, Dr. Ken Gangle, Mr. Richard Parker, Mr. Judd Swihart, and many, many others.

Much of what is good within the following pages is, in part at least, attributable to them. As to the faults, dear reader, they lie not in these "stars" but in ourselves, the authors.

Michael Braun and George Rekers
Gainesville, Florida

THE CONFUSION AROUND US

INTRODUCTION
A PROBLEM OF CONFUSION

A PASTOR'S VIEW

In the past ten years of pastoral ministry I have been gradually led to the uneasy conviction that the "sexual revolution" is a very real challenge to basic human values. We are being caught up in a major cultural upheaval with respect to human sexuality. A virtual sexual eclipse has wrapped our nation in a cloud of confusing darkness. As one would anticipate, since human sexuality is such a pervasive force, any upheaval in our sexual identities is a major upset indeed. It is an upheaval that goes far beyond the vague and sometimes contradictory demands of "gay liberation." It exerts an even broader influence than the more detailed agenda of radical feminism. The sexual revolt is rearing its hydra-headed countenance over the widest spectrum of personal concerns in the home, the church, and society at large.

Sexual confusion is a key symptom of this widespread revolt. And all the factors which contribute to this confusion—divorce, desertion, perversion, chauvinism, promiscuity, as well as a host of other things—are actually the weapons of Satan as he battles for the souls of men.

Where there is confusion there is the inevitable insecurity that leads to hostility. Consequently, violence and sexual confusion travel hand in glove amid the rubble of what was once a more cohesive view of human sexuality. In the area of human sexuality we are witnessing psychological violence upon individuals on an unprecedented scale. This violence is swiftly developing a more tangible form after a decade of sexual indulgence. We appear to be growing insensitive to all but the most brutal of stimuli.

Sexual confusion quickly moves to open conflict. Many of the marriage problems that I have counseled over the last ten years resulted from severe confusion regarding sexual roles and proper sexual conduct. There is intense conflict going on in the marriage relationship today, and a good portion of that conflict springs from promiscuous behavior prior to marriage. As with any open conflict, there are the inevitable casualties, the broken lives inside the broken homes, the bruised and guilty survivors of promiscuous practices. And always, there are the children, the innocents, "who do not know their right hand from their left"— the "little ones" who belong to parents too selfish to resolve their difficulties. These are the battered and abused who learn to hate themselves far more than they hate their tormentors. They confront the Christian counselor; he will always see their faces. These become the vulnerable—all too often the easy prey of aggressive homosexuals, or the heterosexual victims of "love" that promises security and acceptance, but delivers only shame and more self-loathing.

And after that? There are the one million or more every year, who never see the light of day in our country—the aborted children, the terminated pregnancies. Each year, worldwide, 50,000,000 babies have their lives ended before they are born. Fiercely scalded through saline injection, ruthlessly dismembered by suction abortion, their lifeless bodies are discarded in the refuse barrels of a thousand hospitals throughout our country. If the Bible has any part of the truth, their silent cries are heard by God. These are the casualties. They are all around us.

A PSYCHOLOGIST'S VIEW

In my clinical training as well as in my experience as a university psychologist, I've been impressed by the devastating, radical changes in sexual roles which have occurred in America over the past thirty years. In the push and shove of these social changes, many kinds of individual problems have cropped up for men, women, and children. Some unresponsive and insensitive husbands have failed to provide their proper masculine leadership in the home. Some women have allowed themselves to be sucked into the resulting vacuum, overstepping a more natural, supportive role in the home. This domestic upheaval has been labeled by many psychologists as the "dominant wife syndrome."

In other cases I've seen emotional or merely materialistic motives woo many mothers of preschool children out of their homes and into the job market. This functional desertion has often caused serious emotional conflicts for their children. I've seen changing values regarding marital fidelity lead to unstable marriages, divorce, psychological and physical child abuse, as well as to deep personality disturbances in the offending and the offended partner. The results of changing values regarding the place of sexual expression have led to ever larger numbers of extramarital sexual relationships, illegitimate births, abortions, and cases of venereal disease. Obviously, sexual conduct is a matter of profound social impact. It is certainly no mere private concern between two consenting adults.

My own professional work has focused in the areas of clinical child psychology and in marriage and family counseling. I'm sure that every psychologist who works in these areas, as well as every pastor who carries a counseling load, has observed the tremendous amount of stress and strain on the American family which has escalated over the past few decades. Those who counsel people in distress have to be impressed by the clear correlation between the accelerating deterioration of the family unit and the major changes that are taking place in our society's conception of the male and female roles. Could it be that the wholesale American abandonment of the God-ordained male and female roles has brought upon our families a destructive force that will ultimately disintegrate marriage and family, if not soon reversed? I believe that the family will self-destruct in direct proportion to its retreat from the biblically defined male and female roles.

We must take a closer look at some of the current rhetoric that threatens to alter our attitudes regarding sexual roles if we are ever to chart a route back to a normal understanding of marriage and family life. Families are no longer as stable as they once were. Marriages are no longer as permanent as they used to be. My colleagues in psychology conduct endless studies documenting this fragmentation of the family in America, but as a Christian it seems to me that we must get at the source of the problem, rather than examining the problem alone.

As the general populace has retreated from the Judeo-Christian world view, which assigns a high value to stable marriage and family life, we have reaped the consequences of individual suffering. Instead of retaining the natural Christian consensus of our society, we are developing a humanistic world view by default. If we are to discover what the male and female roles should be in family life, we must return to a basis for forming values. That basis is the Word of God.

The prevailing majority in my own profession of psychology pretend to be "value free" when they study male and female roles, family life, or marriage. They even pretend to be "value free" when they try to counsel people under stress in these areas. But it is impossible to work in this sensitive arena of sexual morality and personal life without having your values show. By trying to be "value free," most psychologists reveal their value system of materialistic humanism. The Christian must insist that it is immoral to attempt to view a moral situation amorally.

Non-Christian psychologists often encourage their clients to form their own values regarding sexual expression. In so doing, they mistakenly assume that they are providing the most appropriate and sensitive counsel. In reality, they are tacitly creating an impression that the universe was constructed with no moral law inherent to the system. But God has spoken. God has given us explicit instruction as to what his moral laws are. The psychologist who recommends that a person simply define his own sexual values ends up *not* being an advocate of human freedom; instead, he becomes a revolutionary attempting to overthrow the moral laws of God. Instead of being helped, the client is therefore led down a fanciful path of alleged amorality, called "liberation." But instead of offering true freedom, this path can lead only to ultimate personal destruction and social chaos.

A DUAL PERSPECTIVE

And so we write a book together, a pastor and a psychologist. If Tertullian bemoaned any merger between Jerusalem and Athens, what would be his cry against a union of pulpit and couch? We feel the complexity of the situation calls for a joint consideration of the convoluted highways of the sexual revolt. The laboratory and the Scriptures must inform each other more in these days of accelerated knowledge and accelerated rebellion. Further, this is not merely an esoteric question for the scholar. The problem is being faced by the activist, and a good deal of the solution will come from the hearts of those Christians who not only have an "interest" in the question, but also an investment—an investment of life and true concern.

Without apology, then, we offer this to our readers. It is an affirmation of Christian alternatives in an age of sexual eclipse. This is not a definitive work, but we hope many things in it are definite. Our approach is not all-encompassing, but we hope it hits the mark on many occasions. If our work appears "sprawling," well, perhaps it is. But then again, perhaps the extent of the rebellion against God's laws is so pervasive, with regard to human sexuality, that confining discussion to one or two facets of the question would be too great a concession. We leave it to your judgment. Frankly, this book was written more for the sake of conscience than for any other reason. Having raised our voices, we happily await the time when more able minds and pens join our efforts. As these voices join ours, we hope to proclaim a clear and lasting testimony that we have been made and that we remain "in the image and likeness of God."

ONE
COMING UNGLUED:
A Christian Response to
Sexual Inhibitions and
Secular Intimidation

THE BIBLE HAS SOMETHING TO SAY

An oft-quoted anecdote has an elderly woman taking her
pastor to task for preaching on the Ten Commandments. "Don't
bring up these sins," she counseled; "you'll just give people ideas."
Unfortunately, whatever their motives, Christians are often
notorious for their silence on certain issues. Sex is high on the list
of things "not even mentioned among the Gentiles." Recently I
talked with an official from a well-known Christian publishing
house and was told quite frankly that books on sexual problems
were not popular among Evangelicals.

Overcoming sexual inhibition and secular intimidation. Why do
we suffer such difficult problems so silently? Why do we at times
reflect such high anxiety over sexual sins? Could there be a
correlation between our silence and our anxiety? Emphatically,
yes. Sexual "hangups" become painfully obvious in the
Evangelical community when we easily voice our indictment of
immorality—while our explanation of healing and restoration
from sexual sin is often tragically naive and superficial, if voiced
at all. How ironic it is that Evangelicals, who profess the highest
regard for Scripture, neglect the example of Scripture when it
speaks often and specifically of the *dangers* of sexual immorality
and the *clear remedies* available. As our society careens ever
more erratically from the orbit of Christian values, and threatens
to become a truly secular society, now is no time for Christians

to turn to the comfort of euphemism and circumlocution to escape the ravages of the sexual warfare escalating about them. It is time to speak clearly, unashamedly, and without the squeamishness of past generations.

"When we do so," one might ask, "aren't we in danger of attempting to impose Christian values on a non-Christian culture?" In response to this tired accusation, we should consider a few facts. As much as any society can be "Christian," American society is still "Christian." Indeed, most of the civilized world rests on Christian moorings. The framers of the Constitution, the architects of British common law (as well as those behind the establishment of 1500 years of Western law and civilization) never intended questions of social concern to be discussed and resolved without reference to the nature and will of God, as revealed in Scripture.

The cause of much of the confusion and concern in our society today over standards of sexual behavior is the growing insistence by many that we must define and resolve all questions of morality in society without reference to the nature and will of God. Many contend that any effort to tackle the problem of public morality from the standpoint of Christian values would be an "intrusion" on a secular, non-Christian society. But we *are* a "Christian society"!

According to a 1978 Harris Poll and a 1979 Gallup Poll, nine out of ten Americans pray to God.[1] Eight of ten insist that they believe Jesus to be God or the Son of God. In a speech to the graduating class of Trinity Evangelical Divinity School, the editor of *Christianity Today*, Dr. Kenneth Kantzer, pointed out that in 1979, 90 percent of all Americans "favored the Christian religion." Seventy percent of all Americans were church members. (During the Revolutionary War era, less than 10 percent of all Americans were church members, and no more than 20 percent were church members throughout all the nineteenth century.)

Over 50 percent of all Americans claim to have had a "born-again" experience, and at least 40 percent claim the title "Evangelical." Thirty-three percent of our country is willing to confess Jesus Christ as their "only hope of heaven," and a startling 25 percent of all Americans insist that the Bible is inerrant.[2] An advocate of biblical morality would hardly be an intruder into such an environment! Though God does not regenerate societies, American society was founded on Christian values, and a call to return to them is completely in harmony with our principles as a nation, as well as the collective will of a vast number of citizens.

Silence is not golden. When Christians are silent concerning the validity of a moral code built on the revealed principles of Christian faith, because they mistakenly wish to avoid "imposing" their values on a "non-Christian culture," they are granting a non-Christian minority a victory by default. The forces of secularism have sold us a bill of goods, and we often unquestioningly accept it. We abandon prayer in the classroom and remove the Bible from our schools;[3] we eliminate invocations from public functions and allow our major networks to persist in remaining almost totally devoid of God-consciousness. We often remain silent because we are informed that, after all, ours is a secular, non-Christian society. This is not so!

Recently I attended a small luncheon given by one of the hospitals in my community. It had been rumored that this particular hospital led all others in our city in performing abortions. Some of these abortions, the rumors insisted, were performed after the second trimester limits of the Supreme Court's questionable guidelines (set forth in the notorious *Roe vs. Wade* decision of 1973). It seemed natural for me to raise this question during the interaction of the meeting. My naiveté was met with a fierce response.

"How many abortions does this hospital perform each week?" I inquired, after the number of open-heart surgeries was proudly noted.

"I have no idea," came the sarcastic reply, after a heavy silence. "Do you want me to go back and count each one?"

"Well, I would be interested."

"Frankly, I question your motives for asking. You seem intent on embarrassing this hospital. We will perform all the abortions the law will allow, even if that means a hundred each day. I make no apologies for that."

"I am not asking for apologies; as a pastor I am merely concerned with the moral evil of abortion."

"We don't deal in morality here," the hospital administrator said coldly. "And as for you, you should be concerned with the morality of your own flock, not with this hospital."

His point was well made. He felt that Christian morality had no place in a hospital. He resented any attempt I was making to bring such morality into question. I thought long and hard about his insistence that I "tend to the morality of my own flock." For the first time, I think, I understood the defiant cries of the demons to Jesus' sudden appearance. "Let us alone; what have we to do with thee, thou Jesus of Nazareth? Art thou come to destroy us? I know thee who thou art, the Holy One of God" (Mark 1:24).

The demon's point was well made, too. "What are you doing on our turf? Go away." But, like it or not, Jesus was there. And like it or not, world, the Christian must continue to oppose the works of the devil; he must continue to make the presence of Jesus felt in even the darkest corners of human society.

It is past time for Christians to unashamedly call for a return to biblical, Christian values before our society truly becomes a non-Christian society, like those of China, the Soviet Union, Iran, and Cambodia. The greatest violations of human rights, the greatest intrusions on personal values, and the most resistance to freedom of the individual come from these societies who are proud of the fact that they are non-Christian.

Perhaps Christians would be less reluctant to face the various sexual problems in our country and more eager to raise prophetic voices of promise and hope if they reminded themselves of the biblical view of human sexuality. We need to be constantly encouraged that our faith offers a sane, holistic understanding of sex to a confused and fragmented world. The Bible does not repress our sexuality—it protects, preserves, and enhances it. As with every other dimension of our lives, God's Word offers the most satisfying alternative to the destructiveness of sin in the human experience. Christians have viable alternatives. But they had better proclaim them clearly and quickly before our present sexual eclipse deteriorates into total moral eclipse.

THE BIBLE IS NOT AFRAID TO SAY IT

My wife and I agreed from the outset of our careers as parents to teach by precept and example that there is nothing funny or dirty about our bodies or their natural functions. Quickly we expunged from our children's vocabularies the inevitable childish names for such parts and functions. We were very successful. Too successful, in fact. One morning on the way to church one of our children, who at the time was pushing three, loudly proclaimed that our landlady, a saintly widow, to whom we were talking, "had no penis." The elderly woman, upon hearing this, politely ignored the comment. We, with a touch of apoplexy, began to reconsider the appropriate use of euphemisms and the great wisdom in the proverb, "Children should be seen and not heard."

Frankly, I am not of the school that believes that sexual talk is on a par with asking people what they had for breakfast. Nor do I think that euphemisms are necessarily childish. There is a time for frank language and there is a time for delicate speech. The problem is that our society has become so candid and frank in its sexual discussions that some Christians sound ridiculously innocent by comparison.

The Bible, thankfully, does not share our contemporary tastelessness or our reactionary Victorian inhibitions. It speaks seriously and forthrightly about human sexuality. Yet it often exhibits respect and sensitivity. Many authorities hold that Genesis 9 hints at sexual indiscretion on the part of Ham (Gen. 9:22), yet the account avoids unnecessary reportage. Zipporah's anger was far more explicit than the euphemistic reference in Exodus 4:25 would indicate at face value. The delicate phrase "uncover nakedness" of Leviticus 20:17-21 avoids lurid descriptions while speaking forthrightly against sexual abuse. The Bible at times can be very circumspect.

On the other hand, the Bible was forced to address some appalling conditions that existed in its day, some of which seem to be reviving with even greater force in our modern era. On these occasions the Bible was unashamed to address the problem with clear and unequivocal language. Whether in indictments against adultery (Ex. 20:14), incest (Lev. 18:9), bestiality (Lev. 18:23), or homosexuality (Rom. 1:26, 27), God's Word does not mince language. God's people should follow suit.

It has become tragically apparent that we are living in a day in which sexual vice is escalating at an incredible rate. This is not the time for pastors to become squeamish. They must labor at their tasks as communicators so that they can, with appropriate language, unflinchingly bring God's Word to bear on our needs.

Every Christian must realize that, in order to fulfill the Great Commission, he is going to have to come face to face with things that will be greatly distasteful to him. These things must be addressed. These issues must be faced with all the forthrightness of the scriptural model and with all its discretion.

Such forthrightness will rob the world of some of its favorite indictments against the Christian community—namely, that it is naive, prudish, and terribly inhibited. Actually that criticism fits the world far better. What can be more naive than the world's insistence that sexual activity does not mold our character and shape our values within society? Our world abounds with symptoms of sexual repression. Take television, for example. The networks seem unable to address human sexuality without the vehicle of a situation comedy or the fantasy of a soap opera. One shudders at the philosophy of human sexuality which emerges from our little black boxes.

The Bible does not speak to prudes, nor was it written by prudes. God's Word exhibits a balanced and healthy attitude concerning human sexuality.[4] The judgment of God on his creation undergirds the biblical view of sex: "It is good." But, as with all aspects of humanity, sexuality has been stained by sin and must be redeemed. Because of the impact of sin, human sexuality, created by God for man's good, must be restored to its moral base. God's Word restores human sexuality. It preserves and protects it as well. It does so by speaking directly and forthrightly about it. God's people must adopt the same candor if their object is to confront the world with God's saving plan for man.

ISSUES IN PREMARITAL SEXUALITY

A few years back a young man, just out of high school, came into the office with some exciting news. He had only recently become a Christian and he wanted to talk about it. We sat down together and he began to share his particular story of finding the Lord Jesus as his Savior.

"Are you reading your Bible now?" I asked.

"You bet!" he replied enthusiastically.

We spent the next few minutes "clearing up" where Cain's wife came from and how many hours were in a creation day.

My next question was, "Are you praying regularly?"

His answer was far more intriguing than my question. "Sure, my girl friend and I pray together every night before we go to bed."

"Your girl friend?" I put forward cautiously, proud of the restraint that held my voice at a conversational level, while my thoughts were on the level of Mosaic denunciations. "Yeah," he responded, oblivious to any possible contradiction between his profession and his life style, "my old lady."

"Your old lady?" My restraint was beginning to fail me and I knew it.

"Yeah."

"Oh."

"Do you and your girl friend live together?"

"Sure!"

What would your response have been? My response makes up the sum and substance of this next section.

Premarital sex—Highway to happiness or dead end street? It is fashionable to point out that the accepted practice of monogamous marriage, blessed by the church and protected by civil law, is about to join the dinosaur. Along with the extinction of marriage, our Sunday supplements observe, we will also lose the Victorian sanctions against premarital sexual relations and other kinds of sexual experimentation prior to matrimony.

GAMES PEOPLE PLAY. There are various rationales put forward to justify premarital sex. One such rationale is the romantic appeal to love. This argument takes several forms. First we have the ploy made popular by a recent hit song. A line from its saccharine lyrics asks innocently, "How can anything that feels so right be wrong?" One wonders if such a tune was ever sung by those who happily turned on the showers of Auschwitz. Another, more suitable, ploy is the argument that if you are in love and have made a faithful commitment to another person, why stifle that spontaneous expression by meaningless attention to a "piece of paper"? This philosophy is often taught in the moral classrooms of Johnny Carson and Merv Griffin, among others. It is the noble creed of nearly every TV hero this side of John Boy

Walton. Such "faithful commitment," of course, may take a new object of "commitment" each week, but somehow manages to still call itself fidelity.

CONSENTING ADULTS BEFORE A DISSENTING GOD. Another rationale goes something like this: That which takes place between two consenting adults in private is never wrong. (One hopes that does not cover consenting cannibalism, but the advocates of this view are usually quick to confine its "logic" to sexual "preference" only.) The problem is that what two consenting adults do is never completely "in private." There are social implications in the most private of acts. Abortion clinics and the current VD epidemic serve as mute witnesses to this fact. Theologically it is possible to expand objections even further. Acts done in private never merely concern two consenting adults. With the philosopher Bishop Berkeley, we must acknowledge the constant scrutiny of a third party, God. He is the "watcher of men" (see Job 7:17-20). "Before him no creature is hidden, but all are open and laid bare to the eyes of him with whom we have to do" (Heb. 4:13). Two adults may be consenting, but is God?

MAN IS IN THE EYE OF GOD. There is also a very pious defense of premarital sexual involvement. It can best be illustrated if I once again take you back to my office. This time a middle-aged man sought my help in getting his "wife" to come back to him. She had, it seemed, departed with a boyfriend for a long weekend in neighboring Jacksonville. The word "wife" is set off here because, he was quick to admit, she was not legally his wife. The state of Florida does not recognize the so-called "common law" provisions of many states. Such provisions acknowledge the marital status of those who live together for a prolonged period of time (often over seven years) without benefit of clergy. When I pointed out to him his legal situation (in broad terms, since I am no lawyer), he quickly responded with an objection that I have grown accustomed to hearing over the years.

"But, pastor, we are married in the sight of God."

This is an interesting objection. It is an objection that helps us get back on track with a discussion of the biblical control of human sexuality. What does it mean to be married "in the sight of God"? Is it possible to separate God's approval from man's authority in the matter of marriage? Can we justify the propriety of sexual relations without legal marriage vows?

The Bible's objection to extramarital sex. A basic Christian response to promiscuity must rest on at least one very important passage of Scripture. This passage is doubly important, because not only is the teaching from God's Word, but it is a text developed by the Lord Jesus himself. I am referring to Genesis 2:23, 24 (and its reappearance in Matt. 19:5 ff.). "Then the man said, this at last is bone of my bones and flesh of my flesh: she shall be called Woman because she was taken out of Man. Therefore a man leaves his father and his mother and cleaves to his wife, and they become one flesh."

Of such importance is this passage that it is quoted on three separate occasions in the New Testament. It was quoted once by the Lord Jesus in the dual synoptic accounts of Matthew 19:3-12 and Mark 10:2-12, and twice by the apostle Paul in 1 Corinthians 6:16 and Ephesians 5:31.

THE TEACHING: TIMELESS OR TEMPORAL? An initial minor question faces us. Was this comment made by Adam or Moses? Is Genesis quoting Adam or is this Moses' commentary on the event? It seems best to quote John Murray when he insists: "It makes no difference to the inspired and authoritative character of verse 24 whether it is regarded as an interpretive comment of the inspired writer or as a continuation of Adam's own utterance."[5] It is somewhat significant, however, to ask whether this was binding on all men at all times as a creation mandate enjoined on humanity even before the Fall itself, or a command which could possibly modify only a single period of human history.

The question seems best resolved by the words of Jesus, "From the beginning it was not so." This appeal, in both Matthew and Mark, to the "beginning" leads us to the just conclusion that Jesus taught that Genesis 2:24 was an instruction of Adam made in the Garden of Eden at the beginning. As such it should be binding on all men at all times.

THE UNION: ORDERED OR ARBITRARY? From this passage we can observe many truths. First of all, we should consider that marriage was a human institution inaugurated by man under God's tacit approval. This was included in the Scriptures so that it can be seen that marriage is of divine authority and binding on all men in all ages, within every culture. But we should not ignore the fact that it was a human creation. Because something is a human institution, that does not mean that it is any less binding on us in the sight of God. God requires all men to obey the laws of man. From the outset we must acknowledge that if someone is not married in the eyes of man, that person is not married in the eyes of God.

From this passage we are taught that sexual relations between man and woman are to be protected within the boundaries of marriage. The order is undeniable. A man leaves his father and mother. A man "cleaves" (that is, enters into a binding commitment of fidelity) to his wife.[6] And, following the decision and the action of leaving (and following the varied ways in which a given society might join a man and woman in wedlock), finally, after choice and marriage, they "become one flesh." In 1 Corinthians 6:16 it is clear that "becoming one flesh" is the act of sexual consummation. Genesis 2 is equally clear that sexual intercourse is not to be shared before the commitment and social contract of marriage.

THE PROMISE: KEPT OR BROKEN? It is also evident in Genesis 2 that monogamous sexual relationships are what God requires. Promiscuity is not the pattern that God intended. When, a few years back, *Time* quoted Shirley MacLaine as saying that monogamy was not a "natural function," it was revealing her dreadful lack of understanding of the natural order God set up for the human race. It is polygamy and promiscuity that are "unnatural." It is unnatural for men and women to be governed by their passions. Sex is a wonderful servant but a terrible master. And today our society is in great danger of viewing man as a mere psychic extension of his genital organs.

Genesis 2 declares that one man makes a total commitment to one woman. So far, if our math holds up, one and one equals two. Therefore the "two" become "one flesh." One and one equals two, and two goes into one, once! God intended marriage to be monogamous and permanent. And by protecting two people at their most vulnerable point—their sexuality—God enabled the experience of sexual relationship to be enjoyed. "Marriage is honourable in all, and the bed undefiled" (Heb. 13:4, KJV).

The social suicide of infidelity. How important is such a view of marital fidelity? How important is monogamous marriage? How important is it that men view promiscuity and premarital sex as immoral and continue to frown on the very thought of its acceptance? Let's take a look at Genesis 2:23, 24 once again. The utterance of these words by Adam in the garden marks the moment as one of the most significant events in the history of our race. "Therefore a man leaves his father and his mother and cleaves to his wife, and they become one flesh."

PROVIDING A STABLE ENVIRONMENT. In a very real sense this statement is the first great statement of civil law. Prior to this, God had set up certain conditions governing human life on this planet. Among these were ordinances concerning reproduction (Gen. 1:27, 28), preeminence in creation (Gen. 1:26) and obligations in labor (Gen. 2:15). These were all matters handled directly between God and man. These mandates were stamped on the very nature of humanity—extensions of all that was meant by being created in the image of God.

With Adam's statement regarding marriage and mating, we have the fundamental ordinance that establishes human society; and we have the first great social contract binding and protecting human beings born into society. That social matrix, which would inevitably require the control of civil law, was born when Adam declared how a man and woman would come together in marriage. Marriage begins the process which establishes another social unit, another family. Through the creation of human sexuality, God insured the procreation of the race of man. In this way "he made from one every nation of men to live on all the face of the earth" (Acts 17:26). With the institution of marriage, God gave us the initial control of that process.

Societies would proliferate and grow, be nurtured and thrive, on the strength of monogamous marriage, premarital chastity, and marital fidelity. The fact that some great Old Testament men violated these standards (among them, Abraham, Judah, Jacob, David, et al) in no way diminishes the fact that monogamous marriage and premarital chastity were God's accepted plan for human sexuality. The practice of sexual immorality is a testimony to hardened hearts, not to relative values. Joseph's rejection of Potiphar's seductive wife evidenced a knowledge of God's plan (Gen. 39:7-12). Even pagan Abimelech knew of God's plan for proper sexual expression (Gen. 20:1-7).

ASKING FOR TROUBLE. What is to come of a society that rejects such a fundamental requirement for the well-being of its civil order? If men or women will not be encouraged to be faithful and controlled in marriage, the most basic of human contracts, what will be the outcome in a myriad of other social situations? Will a society that encourages promiscuity and adultery produce dependability in all other areas of its interaction? Will a man who is unfaithful to his wife, who treats contemptuously his own family, who puts his sexual passions ahead of duty, honor, and personal integrity, be faithful in commerce, or teaching, or social service?

Though we are often greatly influenced by those forces which are causing the total fragmentation of life in the twentieth century, and are encouraged to believe that a man's moral behavior has no inherent bearing on how he performs social tasks, nevertheless conscience and Scripture will not let us rest with such socially suicidal heresy. It is time to reassert the biblical view of society that requires all of us to assume responsibility for that society. We must once again acknowledge the corporate identity we share, the cause-and-effect umbilical cord that joins all our actions to the well-being of all our neighbors. We must affirm again that human sexuality and marital fidelity strengthen the very fiber of our society.

The response of the world to this argument is sadly predictable. "What repression! What puritanical inhibiting nonsense! Unrestricted sexual expression is necessary to be a fulfilled human being!" So often such protests are stated most loudly by those who, through immoral choices of their own, have broken families, marriages, and the hearts and lives of many children.

Fear is the real culprit. Biblical standards for human sexuality do not repress sexuality; they protect it. Having counseled people with various problems for over ten years, I am convinced that fear is at the heart of many sexual problems: fear and its handmaiden, shame. Fear of inadequacy, fear of competition, fear of comparison, fear of performance failure. We are most vulnerable at the point of our sexuality. Since we live in a culture where sex even sells soap, we are, all of us, on the verge of sexual neurosis. We all have hangups about sex. This is an American way of life. It's not the heritage of our Puritan ancestors, it's a gift from the twentieth-century media merchants. Listen to our music! We sing about nothing but sexual desires and unrequited love. Love has become a way of spelling sex with four letters. Watch our films! Happiness of the "ever after" kind is always defined as finding your sexual partner. This is overtly stated these days, but has been implicit in the movies for years. (Didn't you ever wonder what they did after riding off into the sunset?)

SEX WITHOUT SHAME. The person who denies having sexual hangups in our culture not only has sexual hangups, he also has a hard time telling the truth. Yet God's Word can heal, protect, and preserve human sexuality. Jesus Christ provides ways in which God's people, though they are in the world, do not have to succumb to the world (John 17:14-19). If we dare to live according to the truth of God's Word, if we dare to trust the Lord's encouragement in our premarital chastity and marital fidelity, our sexuality will be saved from the ravages of sin.

It seems to me that this is the force of Genesis 2:25: "And the man and his wife were both naked, and were not ashamed." Two sexual beings living in a conjugal relationship without hangups, without fear, without shame. When we dare to live according to the control of God's Word, sexual repression and inhibition can be brought under control.

I do not know how some commentators can logically conclude that sex was not experienced by Adam and Eve before the Fall. They had the commandment to be fruitful and multiply. They had the equipment to complete the task. And they had the protection of marriage and the blessings of God on their sexuality. They lived as man and wife and were not ashamed. It is sin, not Scripture, that inhibits, makes dirty, and represses human sexuality. God had other plans for man and woman. God intended man and woman to enjoy their sexuality in its fullest expression without fear or shame.

SHAME WITHOUT SEX. How do you view your sexuality? Is sex a gift of God to enjoy within the guidelines of his Word, or is it a thing of fear and shame? God has a way of restoring human sexuality. God has a way of silencing shame. God has a way of conquering fear; "perfect love casts out fear." Through fear and shame, our sexuality retreats and grows dormant.

God's way of sexual restoration is through repentance and belief in his Son. A relationship with Jesus Christ, begun by a prayer of faith, trusting in his life, death, and resurrection, can renew the image of God in your life (Rom. 5:10). An appeal to God to send his Son into your life through the Holy Spirit can begin a process that will rescue your sexuality, no matter how far it has fallen into degradation and abuse. Paul warns us all that "neither the immoral . . . nor adulterers . . . will inherit the kingdom of God." But he quickly comforts us with these great possibilities: "And such were some of you. But you were washed, you were sanctified, you were justified in the name of the Lord Jesus Christ and in the Spirit of our God" (1 Cor. 6:9-11). In Jesus Christ there is a way to be clean and holy. There is a way to be forgiven of sin. In Jesus Christ there is a way to end the shame and defeat of improper sexual expression. In Jesus Christ there is healing and forgiveness, hope, and above all else, there is freedom from fear and a release from shame.

POINT-COUNTERPOINT

George: Mike, why is it that 90 percent of Americans favor the Christian religion, and yet we have an epidemic of venereal disease, a soaring divorce rate, an increase in the number of unmarried mothers, and in general a failure to practice Christian morality?

Mike: It does seem like a case of raging schizophrenia, doesn't it? Actually, this dichotomy between what we profess to believe and the way we behave is a matter for careful study, if not moral indignation. It does not, however, detract from the fact that our society's basic institutions were all founded on Christian principles and on a Christian world view. And so, in that sense, we are a Christian society if we realize that that does not guarantee Christian behavior within that social framework. The great disparity between what we say we believe and the way we behave is a matter of great sorrow for me, but I merely raise the point to keep us from being intimidated—from clearly articulating Christian viewpoints as a solution to social problems.

George: I've noticed in my professional practice that one way in which many Christians are intimidated is by their acceptance of the idea that any kind of sexual conduct between two consenting adults should be legally permissible. But you have argued convincingly against that notion. So where did this idea about consenting adults come from? Why is it so appealing to Christians to buy into that idea?

Mike: I have an interesting theory about this. In a sense I think the advocates of sexual liberation, when appealing to the right of privacy between two consenting adults, are actually victimizing whatever remnant of a collective Christian conscience may be left in our country. Our consciences find the appeal to privacy compelling because of the Christian conviction that sexual matters are delicate and should be protected by privacy. But on the other hand, the advocates of sexual liberation are misdirecting that Christian concern for privacy. They are using it as grounds to justify anything they want to do. In so doing, they deny any social implications of their sexual improprieties. Of course, this is fundamentally opposed to a Christian conscience and a Christian view of human sexuality. But in a sense they are manipulating or victimizing the Christian conscience by subtly appealing to it. Ironically, they are seeking permission to pursue ungodly acts by an appeal to a godly conscience. This is a classic case of wanting to have one's cake and eat it, too.

George: I'd like to react to something else you said, Mike, about sexual hangups and the shame that is usually associated with sexual problems. I'm painfully aware as a psychologist that the modern solution to shame over sexual sin rarely involves any recognition of the need for forgiveness or healing of moral guilt. Instead, psychologists who encounter a client complaining about shame over their sexual conduct would attempt to ameliorate only the guilt feelings themselves. The psychologist might desensitize the person to his anxiety over sexual sin. In fact, modern people go one step further and try to solve this problem of shame over sexual conduct by a psychological ploy or a coverup. Instead of referring to sexual sin, they rename various sexual practices, using terms that are more acceptable and less judgmental. The non-Christian psychologist does this every day in counseling people. Rather than confronting the shame by admitting its source, a "Band-Aid" approach is taken in which only the symptom is treated, rather than the underlying cause.

Mike: Actually, I think there's a twofold danger, isn't there? Such an approach, such a coverup, is really a denial of a fundamental response to a violation of conscience and the laws of God. It's going to create a great deal of human conflict, if we deny a fundamental need. Many psychologists, in ignoring the issue of sin, redefining it and making it more acceptable, are trying to justify it. They are really doing their clients a disservice. And that's a level one danger. The level two danger is that God has clearly said that such behavior is wrong and that he will bring judgment upon it. If we make ourselves ever more insensitive to God's Word on the matter, we're going to be open to a considerable amount of divine correction in terms of judgment that we will not find pleasant at all. In fact, I suggest that God's judgment on sexual sin is taking place in our society right now. I think one of your own professional peers, one of the Menningers, has written a book on the matter of sin, hasn't he, George?

George: Yes, Dr. Karl Menninger of the world-famous Menninger Clinic was so struck by this modern avoidance of the word "sin" and the idea of moral responsibility by the mental health professions that he wrote a book entitled *Whatever Became of Sin?* (New York: Hawthorn Books, 1973).

Mike: It's interesting that we do have a way of getting rid of words that make our theories and attitudes uncomfortable. We can redefine them almost in an Orwellian 1984 sense. Our dictionary of moral terminology is being subtly rewritten. Our next chapter is about the whole issue of the *rhetoric* of revolt.

TWO
THE RHETORIC OF REVOLT:
The Sexual Propaganda of Humanism

The language we use has potential not only for clear communication, but for manipulation and confusion as well. Our words can make a matter clear and manageable or they can keep people from the truth and even lead them into error in a subtle and sometimes almost indetectable way. When the Nixon White House tried its infamous coverup of the Watergate scandal, the press secretary, in the early stages of the discovery that corrupt actions had occurred, flatly denied any misconduct. This was a simple lie. Later, when the lies were revealed to be lies, the secretary made an announcement that his previous explanation was "inoperative." Later still, he tried to convince reporters that his previous statements had been "misspoken."

This is treacherous ground indeed! Whom was the press secretary trying to fool? What is an "inoperative statement"? In this context, of course, it is a lie. Certainly an "inoperative statement" doesn't sound nearly as bad as the admission, "I lied." This is a clear case of manipulation with words. The intention was not to communicate but to cover up, to confuse. Such actions are intensely human, as old as Cain, and obviously wrong. Yet they illustrate more than an attempt to deceive others. In a more cryptic way they are efforts at self-deception.

WORD GAMES BECOME WAR GAMES

If we, through some magical act of verbal coronation, can only give nicer names to our evil actions, then perhaps our actions won't appear as evil as they are. In fact, we may not feel half as guilty when we do them. After a while we might even come to believe that there is nothing wrong with making "inoperative statements." It would be harder to convince ourselves that there is nothing wrong with *lying, dishonesty* and *deception.* If we identify these acts with their proper titles we become painfully aware that they should never be "operative."

Through the magic of "redefinition," old sins become "viable alternatives." By simply relabeling things with nicer names, we can feel a lot better about doing them. If someone wants to revolt against the moral standards of honesty, it is not likely that he will crusade with a banner saying, "Lies Are Beautiful." He needs a word that sounds much nicer than "lie."

Sexual behavior today is a battlefield in which the word games are in fact war games. If someone wants to pursue an immoral sexual life, it should not be surprising that he would try to rename his actions to make them sound nicer. We haven't found anyone who has crusaded with the slogan, "Sexual Sin Is Beautiful." That would be too blatant. But if we could only think of new names for immoral actions, our result would not be so obvious. The easiest way to break moral standards is to develop a "rhetoric of revolt."

Let's pretend for a minute that you are going to plan a sexual revolt. One of your first obstacles would be a whole slew of words in the English language which refer to immoral sexual actions. There are nasty-sounding words such as perversion, pornography, prostitution, permissiveness, fornication, adultery, vice, and homosexuality. The first step of revolt would be to find newer, nicer-sounding words for these age-old sins.

PRESTO—CHANGEO!

Perversion becomes an "alternate life style." The word "perversion" implies that there is a normative standard which can be perverted. The normal marriage relationship of a man and a woman has been recognized by God as the proper standard. Men have rightly concluded that any deviation from this standard is a perversion. Anyone who deviates from a moral standard has been called a deviate or a pervert. These are strong words which imply a definite moral standard. However, if we can pretend for a minute that sexual behavior exists in a moral vacuum, then we can take the liberty of substituting for *these* words, with such strong moral connotations, *other* words, which imply some kind of optional choice.

For example, if a person has a sexual relationship with an animal, in a moral vacuum you might call that behavior a "sexual variation" instead of a "sexual perversion." If a man has promiscuous homosexual relationships with a long series of other men, we could refer to that pattern as an "alternate life style"—if we live in a moral vacuum. Certainly, "alternate life style" sounds a lot nicer than "perverted life style" or "living in sin."

If there are no moral standards in the universe which pertain to sexual behavior, then we can easily substitute much nicer-sounding words like "variation," "alternate life style" or "alternate adaptation," for the old term, "sexual perversion."

Pornography becomes "sexual realism." Certainly "sexual pornography" has a nasty ring to it. The whole concept of obscenity implies that there is some moral standard of decency and propriety. The United States Supreme Court has defined obscene material in terms of "community standards"; but in a moral vacuum, eventually "anything goes." If no standards exist, then the portrayal of explicit nonmarital sexuality in magazines and films can be seen as "realism." After all, doesn't "realism" sound much nicer than "pornography"? Who can be against reality? But the problem with pornography is that it is *not* realistic, because it portrays supersexed men and women who rarely suffer any adverse effects of their sexual escapades, such as VD, depersonalization, or guilt.[1]

If there are no moral standards that exist in reality, then explicit portrayals of sexuality are "realistic," and pornography disappears. Why, for example, would we need to protect children from "reality"? It would be easier to justify the public distribution of a photograph of a sexual act between a man and a boy if we called it "realism" than if we called it by the older name of "pornography."[2]

It is not surprising, is it, that theaters which market pornography do not call themselves "pornography theaters"? Oh, no! They are "adult theaters."

Prostitution becomes "surrogate therapy." There are many unmarried men who rebel against the Bible's counsel to be chaste. Calling themselves "unfulfilled," they purchase the services of a female sex partner who is called a "surrogate" in a "professional" service called sex therapy. From a moral frame of reference, paying for sexual relations is called prostitution. In fact, there are certain social activists who are pressuring for legislation to allow legalized prostitution. But the general public is largely turned off by the negative-sounding word "prostitution."

How could this practice be raised to a more dignified level that would sound more respectable? A solution has been found by some "liberation" advocates. Using the nicer-sounding words of the "health professions," certain marriage counselors and doctors have introduced a version of sex therapy in which a sexual partner is provided money to perform as a "therapy surrogate." Such a program administered by doctors for the purpose of "therapy" to a person with a "sexual problem" certainly sounds a lot more respectable than prostitution. Many of these "professionals" are lobbying for state legislatures to revise laws to allow payment for sexual relationships which are "under the direction of a licensed therapist." Thus an action which may only look sleazy and immoral in a brothel may gain a certain respectability in the confines of a doctor's office.

Permissiveness becomes "sexual freedom." The word "permissiveness" has a negative ring to it because it implies an indifference to or outright breaking of certain clear moral standards. In a moral vacuum, we can simply rename promiscuous and perverted sexual behavior as "sexual freedom." In twentieth-century America, we all admire a person who is "free of hangups."[3] Now we can speak of a person being free of sexual hangups if he can emerge guilt-free from numerous types of sexual escapades.[4] Under the banner of "freedom," any advocate for overthrowing sane standards of sexual behavior sounds almost patriotic—a loyal American.

Premarital relations become "trial marriages." Words like
"adultery" and "fornication" imply a serious transgression against
a moral law.[5] But if we can adopt the frame of reference which
eliminates such restrictive moral standards, we can use newer and
nicer-sounding words like "trial marriage." "Marriage" is a time-
honored tradition, after all, and since we are used to "trial offers"
on all kinds of merchandise, doesn't it make perfect sense to
advocate "trial marriage"? In fact, this new term implies that the
couple is much smarter than the rest of us because they are
trying something out first to see if it works.

Maybe we would only be troublemakers if we pointed out that
advocates of a "trial marriage" are entering into a relationship
without a firm commitment. In the absence of the firm
commitment, the relationship is less likely to last, so the "trial" is
not really given a fair chance. The word "trial marriage" quietly
and effectively undermines the cardinal principle of marriage—
permanent fidelity. One wonders if such trial marriages produce
"trial children" and "trial parents." One does not build a
meaningful life on a "trial" principle. Whenever I fly in an
airplane I do not want to be told that my pilot is a "trial
aviator." My life is more important to me than that. So is my
marriage.

The main point, however, is that a new word like "trial
marriage" is so much more high-sounding, and if advocates can
only get society to stop using terms such as "living in sin" or
"adultery," they can perhaps convince people that we *do* live in a
moral vacuum after all.

Profanity becomes "freedom of speech." Some people complain
about the use of sex to market everything from automobiles to
men's aftershave lotion. In a moral framework, our sensibilities
might be offended, but with the idea that all moral values are
relative (a destructive, but common idea), we would relabel this
whole issue a matter of "freedom of speech." Off-color jokes,
pornographic images and sexual immorality on television can all
be defended in an amoral universe under the very patriotic
banner of freedom of speech.

Lies become "sexual liberation." Propaganda for the elimination
of standards of sexual behavior can have a legitimate sound to

them if we combine the cause with the word "liberation."[6]

Name-calling is often an effective strategy for getting someone to break down his or her moral standards. For example. if you call someone a "sexist" when he advocates legitimate distinctions between men and women, you have undermined a certain amount of the legitimacy commonly granted to that moral standard. If you combine the name-calling strategy with the relabeling word game, you can make sexual perversion sound laudable. This is why some homosexual activists call themselves members of a "gay liberation" group who fight against "bigots" who hold onto moral standards for sexual behavior. These homosexual activists attempt further to dignify their status by calling themselves a "minority group." They hope to share the sympathy extended by a compassionate society to the victims of blind prejudice. In one fell swoop, this particular word game transforms a "pervert" to a noble member of the "oppressed" and transforms the spokesman for morality into an immoral advocate of "bigotry."

People who want to eliminate the distinctions between men and women would make a strategic blunder if they called themselves advocates of an "anti-sex" movement. Instead, they pick a word such as "unisex," which is a strange bit of nonsense, evidently implying that sex docsn't matter. However, the common man will not notice the logical absurdity of such a word. You can get away with a great deal if you use words that sound halfway respectable. There may be another coverup taking place that would make Watergate look like a tea party.

Abortion becomes "terminated pregnancy," death becomes "liberty." Radical feminists advocate universal access to 100 percent federally funded abortions as a means of implementing their goal of equalizing women with men.[7] They contend that this would free women from the "burden" of childbirth.[8] Instead of talking about the death of the unborn child, these groups talk about "termination of the pregnancy" or the "right to choose." This quickly shifts attention away from the fact that a human life has been willfully destroyed.

Instead of conceptualizing abortion as killing a developing human life, radical feminists and other advocates reconceptualize this murderous event as simply the "right" of a woman to control "her own body."[9] By shifting focus away from the killing of an unborn child and onto "the pregnancy" or "the mother's body," they make the procedure sound more acceptable.[10]

Instead of talk about the woman's "right to kill her unborn child," there is talk about a fuzzy concept of the "equal rights of the woman," which almost sounds believable as long as one doesn't think about it very carefully. Somehow a woman's "rights" to "equality" demand that she be able to go through life without the "burden" of bearing a child, in the same way that men do not have the burden of bearing a child. The idea that men and women could ever be biologically equal with respect to bearing children is ridiculous, if not impossible to imagine. Still, the words "right" and "equality" sound so much better than "murder."

It seems almost un-American to deprive someone of her "rights" to be "equal." But equal to what? Men are not granted the equal right to decide whether or not a pregnancy resulting from their intercourse should be terminated. Do men have the "equal" right to kill an unborn child that they helped conceive if the mother wishes to have that baby? Why then does our society allow the mother the *unequal* right to kill the fetus, which was equally the product of the father's sperm and the mother's egg?

The battle of words is over if humanistic thinkers succeed in getting people to see the murder of unborn children in new terms such as the "rights" of a woman over her own body. The battle has been lost if we find ourselves thinking about "terminated pregnancies" instead of mourning for a murdered human life.[11]

SEXUAL RELATIVISM IS OPEN REVOLT

Today we find sex education curriculum used in the public schools which refers to homosexuality and sexual deviations as "alternate life styles." Abortion is seen as an "alternative birth control method." Do not be surprised if you hear "infanticide" labeled as a "family planning" method. (You may even have supported such things by gifts to Planned Parenthood through the United Way.) The assumption of many sex educators is that moral teaching should be left to the home and the church while information in school should be presented "objectively," that is, in a moral vacuum. As a result, a strong value position is taken in these materials which legitimates deviant sexuality as a "variation" or an "alternative" which it is up to the individual to choose. By placing sexual behavior in an amoral setting, the writers produce materials which are tacitly immoral in their recommendations.

Many psychologists and psychiatrists are now taking the same relativistic approach to the therapy of people with homosexual behavior. Because some of these therapists view homosexual behavior as merely a "variation" instead of a "perversion," the therapist will offer the homosexual assistance in being a "more effective homosexual" and to eliminate guilt feelings for homosexual behavior and orientation.[12] These same therapists will question the ethics of other therapists who try to help homosexuals eliminate their deviant behavior and orientation.

When Dr. Alfred Kinsey of Indiana University published his landmark survey reports on sexual behavior[13] in the late 1940s and early 1950s, many people interpreted his statistics in a moral vacuum. Taking a relativistic approach, people would reach surprising conclusions from reading Kinsey's reports. Because Kinsey found that roughly 1/3 of all men participated in homosexual behavior at least once after puberty, some people considered this a "norm" which implied a positive value for homosexual behavior. Rather than comparing their own behavior to a moral standard, they would compare their behavior to these Kinsey statistics. For a person in sexual revolt, this is a tempting strategy.

Somehow it is comforting to know that other people have participated in the same behavior. If Kinsey had studied the incidence of lying behavior, he might have found that 99 percent of all people have lied in their adult lives (assuming a 1 percent error variance). If we could only call dishonesty an "alternate life style" and compare our behavior to such statistical "norms" instead of comparing our behavior to some moral standard, we could do away with the concept of "sin" altogether.

THE RELIGION OF HUMANISM

Why do people want to change the words that we use to describe sexual normality and sexual abnormality? Why do people want

to abandon the language of normal heterosexuality? Why do the
radical feminists want to obliterate the meaning of masculinity
and femininity and abolish the institution of marriage?[14] Some do
so for strategic purposes—these are the propagandists. Many
more do so from conflicts within themselves, conflicts of which
they are only vaguely aware.

Motivations to view sexuality in one way or another are
determined by a person's world view. By way of explanation, let's
indulge in some simplistic models of communication. One might
suggest that there are two basic world views. There is the theistic
view with God at the center, or there is the materialistic view
holding that the universe emerged from and continues according
to impersonal forces. These world views are supported by one of
two basic value systems, either an objective system or a subjective
system. The objective system draws its knowledge from the facts
of God's revealed Word, the objective truths of science, history,
and experience. The subjective system draws its knowledge
primarily from conscience or whatever arbitrary authority appeals
to the person.

The word games that are played in the rhetoric of sexual revolt
are motivated by humanistic and/or materialistic beliefs.
Interestingly enough, many clever word games arise from the sad
combination called "Christian humanism." This is a thinly
disguised version of humanism which cannot logically be called
"Christian," but the humanistic word game strategists know that
the word "Christian" connotes positive emotional feelings to
many people. They would like to legitimate humanism by using
"Christian" as an adjective. But logically, the terms "Christian"
and "humanism" are in opposition. Christianity rests on an
objective system of values, while humanism rests on subjective
values. Though the term "Christian humanism" is self-destructive,
its short-lived existence will be the source of boundless confusion.
Misguided Christians who attempt to salvage values from their
inner selves with the moorings of God's revealed truth—the
Scriptures—are headed for an inevitable collision with the law of
God.

In the twentieth century, we have witnessed a large increase in
the number of individuals who have adopted this materialistic
world view called humanism. Humanism is a radical attempt to
redefine morality. Americans, long applauded for their pragmatic

FIGURE I

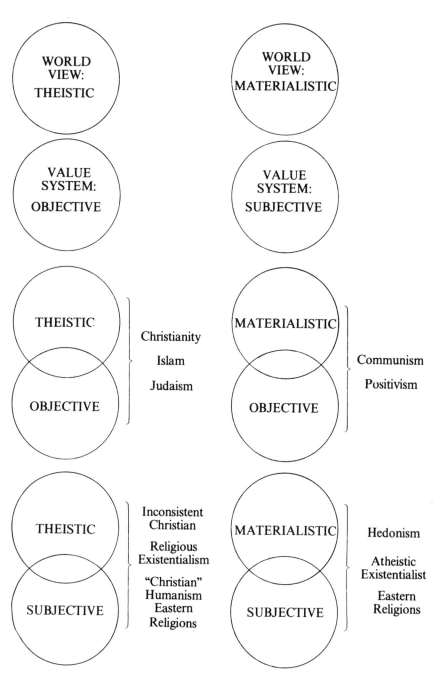

eclecticism, are now suffering from the moral delusions of
humanistic Christianity or a Christianized humanism. The two
world views are sworn enemies of each other.[15] When merged
together, the utilitarian strategy of humanism is served well, but
the heart of Christianity is ripped out.[16]

What is humanism? According to the *Humanist Manifesto,*
"Humanism is a philosophical, religious, and moral point of view
as old as human civilization itself."[17]

In 1933, "a group of thirty-four liberal humanists in the United
States defined and enunciated the philosophical and religious
principles that seemed to them fundamental. They drafted
Humanist Manifesto I, which for its time was a radical
document. It was concerned with expressing a general religious
and philosophical outlook that rejected orthodox and dogmatic
positions. . . .[18]

"*Humanist Manifesto I,* important as it was in its time, has
since been superseded by events; though significant, it did not go
far enough. It did not and could not address itself to future
problems and needs. In recognition of the pressing need for a
new, more relevant statement, 40 years later, *Humanist Manifesto
II* was drafted."[19]

THE SEXUAL INTEREST OF HUMANISM. It is not surprising that
such important aspects of human life as sexuality, reproduction,
child rearing, and sexual roles would be a prime target for
anyone hoping to create a new moral point of view. The values
behind the laws or regulations that society sets up must be
derived from world-view belief systems. The *Humanist Manifesto I*
recognized this in stating that "religions have always been means
for realizing the highest values of life," and ". . . religion itself
remains constant in its quest for abiding values, an inseparable
feature of human life."[20] However, the *Humanist Manifestos*
propose "radical changes in religious beliefs" that govern the
important areas of human life.

What are the basic beliefs of humanism? This world view can
best be understood by reading direct quotations from the
Humanist Manifesto II.[21]

HUMANISM VS. THEISM. Humanist religion does not attempt to
simply reinterpret traditional religion, but to radically propose an
atheistic belief.[22]

"We find insufficient evidence for belief in the existence of a supernatural; it is either meaningless or irrelevant to the question of the survival and fulfillment of the human race. As non-theists, we begin with humans, not God, nature not deity."[23]

HUMANISM AND MORAL ANARCHY. On the subsection of "Ethics," the *Humanist Manifesto II* sets forth the principles upon which humanists decide what is right and wrong.

"We affirm that moral values derive their source from human experience. Ethics are *autonomous* and *situational*, needing no theological or ideological sanction. Ethics stem from human need and interest. . . . We strive for the good life, here and now."[24]

In the subsection entitled "The Individual," the *Humanist Manifesto II* directly states the humanistic view of human sexuality:

"We believe in maximum individual autonomy consonant with social responsibility. Although science can account for the causes of behavior, the possibilities of individual *freedom of choice* exist in human life and should be increased."[25]

This is a far cry from the word "humanism" (small "h") which has come to describe all that is good and assertive of human dignity. Such a romantic definition of "humanism" is quickly shown up for what it is when one asks for its antonym. Humanism (small "h" or big "H") stands opposed to any system of values which emerge from any source other than man.[26] Humanism is diametrically opposed to any value system or belief system that is God-centered. Humanism is not merely a study of man and his concerns; it is a study of man without God. Though the word "humanism" is often misunderstood and misapplied, and though such a misunderstanding is welcomed by humanists, its secular essence is clear to any open mind.

HUMANISTIC WORD GAMES: The humanist has some definite views of human sexuality:

"In the area of sexuality, we believe that intolerant attitudes, often cultivated by orthodox religions and puritanical cultures, unduly repress sexual conduct. The right to birth control, abortion, and divorce should be recognized."[27]

". . . neither do we wish to prohibit, by law or social sanction, sexual behavior between consenting adults. The many varieties of sexual exploration should not in themselves be considered 'evil.'"[28]

Here we see the origins of the "rhetoric of sexual revolt."

Instead of making reference to perversion, pornography, prostitution, premarital sex, adultery, fornication, or murder of unborn children, this statement uses such doctored terms as "freedom of choice," "sexual behavior between consenting adults," "sexual exploration," "sexual proclivities," and "life styles."

Although there are many statements in the *Manifesto* that could be commonly accepted, such as the call for courage, intellectual achievement, the controlled use of scientific methods, humility, reason, human caring, problem solving, love, creativity, and social responsibility, it is the entire framework or world view that must be comprehended and accepted or rejected as a whole. Other world views, such as the Judeo-Christian world view, also promulgate these qualities of love, creativity, reason, and the like. However, the Christian view is set in an entirely different framework.

The moral relativism of humanistic religion. According to the humanistic world view, ethical choices are not based on the *intent*, or on the action itself; rather, a "good or bad" choice is determined on the basis of the *consequence* for the individual or for society. For the individual, the humanistic goal is for "self-actualization" and for the "greatest happiness." For society, the ethical goal is for social utility.

This means that the framework for ethical decision-making in the humanistic system demands that all values are *relative*. With no source of abiding moral principles, ethics become simply *situational*. Beliefs and values are determined by the humanist, to fulfill individual needs and interests and the pragmatic needs for society. Therefore, ethical decision-making is an *autonomous* process, which means that the individual's moral choice must be justified to himself only. Self-justifying ethical decisions are not based on any universal principles or rules that would transcend time or a particular culture. What is "right" at one time and in one culture according to self-justification may be "wrong" at another time and in another culture. Without an independent standard such as the Ten Commandments, *murder* might be justifiable in one situation and considered "right" by one set of individuals, whereas at another time and another place it might be considered "wrong."

One of the best ways to grasp the drastic contrast between

humanism and Christianity is to compare this humanistic process of moral decision-making to the theistic world view. Moral and ethical standards for choices within the theistic world view are based upon universal principles revealed by God directly in Scripture and intended for teaching in the home and the church. The Christian world view acknowledges the existence of a personal, just, and loving Creator God, who seeks a direct relationship with individuals who are created in his image. Those individuals therefore possess the potential for ultimate meaning and purpose in life. Those who freely choose to relate to God in faith and righteous living are provided not only a set of universal moral standards by which to live, but also the direct assistance from God to make moral choices. Therefore, the Christian world view provides a frame of reference for ethical decision-making which is not merely relative or situational. In the Christian framework, the ethical decision cannot be autonomous or merely self-justifying.

For example, in an overpopulated world, a humanistic framework might allow the killing of young children. This would be an option, if it served the social utility of reducing population size, particularly if these children were labeled "undesirable" because of physical handicaps or mere differences in features. But in the Christian world view, there would never be any situation or relative circumstance in which the killing of young children would be justified. The moral absolute delivered by God teaches that murder is always wrong, no matter at what time or in what culture. A supernatural frame of reference is necessary in order to have absolute moral principles which transcend time and particular culture.

This example is not very far removed from present reality in the world. At this juncture in history, each person faces two fundamental options: (1) to accept the humanist's world view or (2) to reject it in favor of a theistic world view and the Christian ideals of sanctity of life, selfless love, and service of God and others. The accumulation of individual value choices will determine the destiny of our culture. The humanistic choice involves sexual revolt from the ideal of normal heterosexual roles. On the other hand, the Christian choice involves the acknowledgment of transcendent moral values which specify a norm for sexual behavior, heterosexual roles, and family life.

We must recognize the humanistic word games for what they are—merely a rhetoric of revolt against God's moral law.

POINT-COUNTERPOINT

Mike: George, we have moved from a defense for the traditional Christian view of morality in sexual conduct, set forth in chapter one, to an analysis, in chapter two, of the contemporary assault upon that basic biblical view of human sexual morality. In this assault the first strategy has been to attack the roots of morality through the various word games that you delineated so well. Following that, the prevailing Christian world view has to be replaced with a basic secular philosophy, namely, humanism. Chapter two seems to outline this evolution quite well. But there is one more step that I think remains, and that is to galvanize the philosophy into radical action—from random rebellion against a standard, toward consistent revolution.

George: I think you're right, Mike. We have noted that the modern revolt against God's standard for sexuality and God's standard for men and women's roles begins with a clever change of words to make that revolt more palatable. Now we need to move on from exposing that philosophy to take a critical look at the actions which follow from that atheistic way of thinking. Psychologists for a long time have been keenly interested in the relationships between people's thinking or beliefs and their actual behavior.

Mike: It does seem that the 1980s will be unique in that we will finally see what has been a common anti-Christian philosophy become crystallized into definite anti-Christian plans of action. And as we go into the next chapter, we will discover that much of the radical feminism that is challenging traditional sexual models is essentially a crystallizing of anti-Christian sentiment into an amoral social framework.

George: I think if we look at history, the first anti-Christian sentiment that was worked out into action was male chauvinism. Historically, that happened first, and that definitely is an anti-

Christian approach. More recently we've seen a plan of action on the other end of the spectrum called feminism or radical feminism.

Mike: In a sense, vague skirmishes are now resolving into major battle fronts. The battle lines are being drawn.

THREE
DRAWING THE BATTLE LINES:
The Radical Challenge
of Sexual Extremists

There is much to commend in the feminists' complaint:

"Whatever women do they must do twice as well as men to be thought half as good. Luckily, this is not difficult."

This humorous quote from the ubiquitous philosopher, "Anonymous," strikes a familiar chord in the minds of many. Unfortunately, the sarcasm is all but lost on the inflexible male chauvinist. Its humor is apparent only to those who are willing to admit that women are often victims of injustice in our society. Ironically, the tragic battle between intransigent chauvinism and inflexible feminism bought the laughter for this not-so-funny one-liner. Male chauvinism and radical feminism are two vocal expressions of sexual extremism found in twentieth-century America. Both viewpoints stand contrary to God's purpose. They are opposite sides of the same coin of sexual revolt. The lines are drawn and the battle is raging.

MALE CHAUVINISM

History has witnessed many examples of a distortion of male leadership into an oppressive tyranny in which men have degraded the dignity of women and abused their human rights.

Historical examples of the illegitimate wielding of leadership power, of course, do not logically lead us to abandon the male leadership role in the church and in the home. But careful attention must be directed at the existence of illegitimate masculine manipulation which is referred to as "male chauvinism."

One area in which males have illegitimately dominated has been the area of employment and the marketplace. There is no justification for women being given unequal pay for an equal job performed in the professions and other employment settings. Only an attitude of unjust discrimination, which is the hallmark of male chauvinism, would pay a woman $12,000 a year for performing the identical job that a man performs for a salary of $25,000 a year.

Male chauvinism is an arrogant, unloving, and unfairly discriminatory attitude in which males automatically consider women inferior or less than fully human.

There are some laws which reflect a male chauvinistic attitude which need to be revised by state legislatures. For example, a man can divorce his wife on the grounds of drunkenness and adultery in some states in which it is impossible for the woman to divorce her husband on the same grounds.[1]

Another example of incipient chauvinism can be found in the various contradictory state laws governing inheritance. For example, some state laws hold that if a husband owns a farm and dies, his widow must pay an inheritance tax. But if the wife dies, the husband pays no such inheritance tax.[2]

In some cases, a male chauvinistic attitude has worked against or discriminated against men themselves. For example, many state laws were formulated with the attitude that men are always the aggressor in initiating sexual activity. Although psychological evidence suggests that this may be the case in the majority of instances, it certainly is not always true. The stereotype is misleading. However, a male chauvinistic attitude would always view the woman as the victim and the man as the perpetrator of sexual crimes. For example, according to most state laws, the following paradox occurs. Laws are set up such that if a *woman* happens to undress in front of an open window, and a man stops to look at her, the *man* could be arrested for being a Peeping Tom. But in the reverse situation, if a man undressed in front of an open window, and a woman stopped by to look at him, the man could be arrested for indecent exposure.

Our speech reveals a great deal both by design and by unconscious reflex. Many an old "battle axe" has been caught standing in a Freudian slip. As the apostle Peter blew his cover because of a Galilean accent, and a hostile member of the crowd yelled triumphantly, "Thy speech betrayeth thee," so all too often men are guilty of speaking in the purest form of "Chauvinese."

Men speak with pride of their car and sometimes let the "little woman" use it. (I once knew a husband who gallantly opened "his car" door in order to "put his wife in"). Men speak of "my" house, yet expect the wife to clean it like a good housewife should. Many men will lament the fact that so much of their money is spent on *her* grocery bills. Men are not always inflexibly possessive. "My son" quickly becomes "your kid," if problems arise. Chauvinese is spoken most clearly in many an American home, which, after all, is "a man's castle." A father often lets the family read "his paper" after he is finished. Occasionally he will spend an evening with the family around "his TV," provided that Dad selects the programs. There are, to be sure, certain rooms within the "man's castle" that have been nobly given to the woman. Usually among these are the kitchen, sewing room, bathrooms, and of course, the laundry room. The husband, on the other hand, may choose to relax in "his den," "his study," or busy himself in "his workshop."

Chauvinese is spoken outside the home as well. On the way to the office, men may curse the antics of "woman drivers" and expect the instant recognition of a number of stereotypical generalizations. The corollary "man driver" lacks any substance whatsoever in Chauvinese. Arriving at the office, he will say "Good morning" to the "girls" who work for him, and refuse the promotion of some because he knows that "most men wouldn't be caught dead working for a woman." Our boss knows he must find the "right man for the job."

The fact is, Chauvinese is spoken worldwide. In Chauvinese

"women doctors" are always noted while "male doctors" sounds redundant. All doctors readily treat any who are afflicted with "female disorders" while a male disorder lacks medical definition. In reality, Chauvinese makes the world a very simple place. Women are easily divided into simple categories such as "foxes," "chicks," or "kittens" if desirable, and "pigs," "cows" or "real dogs" if less than desirable. A "real dog" is usually someone with "a face like a horse" but shouldn't be confused with the attractive young woman who is a "cute little filly." Unfortunately, "cute little fillies" when married often turn into "old nags." This is a dilemma to some men who see themselves as "real studs." In the uncomplicated world of Chauvinese, men never "get into tizzies," or "worry their pretty little heads." One rarely mistranslates Chauvinese. For example, we all know who does and who does not qualify for the title "dumb blonde," and we generally understand why they "have more fun."

Male chauvinism is an attitude which would automatically expect the female to be generally inferior to the male in any task or function without evaluating the individual woman's actual capabilities. For many years in the United States, the attitude of male chauvinism resulted in women not being allowed to vote, to own property, or to earn a college degree. Fortunately, a constitutional amendment was passed which enfranchised women so that now they have equal opportunity at the polls. With only a few minor exceptions, which are being rapidly corrected by state legislatures, women now have equal rights and equal opportunity in America to engage in business contracts, to receive every level of education from kindergarten to Ph.D. programs, to have equal access to employment opportunities and compensation, and to pursue any employment without discrimination.

Although the mark of male chauvinism is being conscientiously removed from the American legal system and from American government, its existence has unfortunately provided the fuel for the proponents of the opposite destructive force known as "radical feminism." Although male chauvinism is wrong and certainly far more pervasive than its counterpart, radical feminism, the sad truth remains that radical feminism is potentially more destructive because of the female's key role in providing personal, psychological, and social stability.[3]

RADICAL FEMINISM

Radical feminism is a dangerous form of revolt which is equally as wrong as male chauvinism. Radical feminism is a symptom of major revolt in itself and often uses examples of male chauvinism as convenient excuses to rationalize its own destructive course of action. The impact of radical feminism upon American life can be understood by considering, first, its overriding philosophy. We will inspect the 1972 *Declaration of Feminism* as a cogent summary of this world view. Moving from that, we should observe how this philosophy is translated into political demands. The *Plan of Action* adopted by the 1977 National Women's Conference affords us that opportunity. A final consideration would be how radical feminists intend to implement their political strategies. A survey of the ERA question and an example of Florida feminist lobbying can well illustrate the feminist approach to political activism.

In discussing radical feminism, it is our intention to distill under one heading the most popular tenets of the extreme women's rights activists. Not all feminists share each view here discussed, but to the extent that they do they become, in our opinion, unwitting servants of an extremely malevolent contemporary social force. In our opinion, the radical feminist tends at times to be more logically consistent than the more moderate feminist who parrots a radical strategy while being committed to more stable social values. The radical feminist tends to see sexual inequality as merely a symptom of our totally corrupt economic and political system, while the moderate feminist may only be concerned with righting the immediate wrongs of sexual inequality. We do not wish to oppose every feminist, but we would counsel each feminist to examine the full logical, moral, and theological implications of her position.

A declaration of revolt. One way to document the extreme philosophy of radical feminism is to let the radical feminists speak for themselves . . .

On sexuality, the philosophy of radical feminism declares: "Heterosexual relationships are by their very nature oppressive to women in the male dominated society. Liberated sexuality is freedom from repression of sexual needs and desires."[4]

The radical feminist philosophy is opposed to traditional marriage: "The end of the institution of marriage is a necessary condition for the liberation of women. Therefore, it is important for us to encourage women to leave their husbands and not to live individually with men. We must build alternatives to marriage."[5] Obviously, such views on sex and marriage would throw radical feminists into direct conflict with the traditional structures of family life and child rearing. The radical feminists gladly accept the challenge of attempting to overthrow these fundamental social institutions.[6]

On the topic of an overall platform for feminism, the manual of the National Organization for Women (NOW), entitled, "Revolution: Tomorrow Is NOW,"[7] includes the following major points:

1. Government funding for day-care centers.
2. Positive attitudes toward lesbians and pro-lesbian legislation.
3. Free abortion, sterilization, and contraception.
4. The elimination of tax exemptions for churches.
5. The removal from schools of textbooks which portray women in the role of housewife or mother.
6. Requiring schools to provide sex education, contraceptives, abortion counseling, and women's liberation programming.
7. Eliminating women's exemption from the draft.

Plan of action. A good way to understand how the radical feminist philosophy is translated into specific action is to consider some of the proposals that came out of the National Women's Conference[8] (November 18-21, 1977, in Houston, Texas).

The "National Plan of Action" adopted by the National Women's Conference reflects many of the major tenets of radical feminism.[9] The expressed goal of the *National Plan of Action* is to implement its planks as public policy through political action. Let's look at four of the proposals of this plan.

ABORTION ("REPRODUCTIVE FREEDOM"). The officially published

National Plan of Action was stated as a "demand" for "immediate and continuing action" to be taken "by Federal, State, public and private institutions" on a number of proposals, including one on "Reproductive Freedom" (cited verbatim in the footnotes).[10] This proposal asks that federally funded abortion-on-demand be made available to every American woman of any age at any stage of pregnancy.

This proposal also includes federally funded family planning services which would be confidential for all recipients, including teenagers. This means the federal government would tax parents in order to provide contraceptives and abortion to their own children, whether the parents wanted it or not. In fact, the government would insure that parents need never know of their child's decisions.

The concept behind this proposal, as presented at the National Women's Conference, is that "reproductive freedom" furthers woman's "equality" by relieving her of the burden of carrying children. The "relief" of this burden is to be funded completely by the taxpayer.

HOMOSEXUALITY ("SEXUAL PREFERENCE"). Another demand made by the *National Plan of Action* of the National Women's Conference was a proposal[11] which would require the federal, state, and local governments to remove any limits on openly avowed and practicing homosexuals to marry and to adopt children. This proposal also would guarantee the "right" of openly practicing homosexuals and bisexuals to teach children and the "right" to present homosexuality, bisexuality, or bestiality as a normal, acceptable "alternative life style" in any state or federal institution such as a child-care center, juvenile shelter, counseling clinic, or school. This proposal would require the federal government to eliminate all legal barriers that exist against any sexual deviation by any individual. It would, of course, mean that openly practicing homosexuals, sadomasochists, pedophiliacs, and those engaging in bestiality would not only have the right to adopt children but to teach children in public and private schools. They would be free to teach them that these various sexual perversions are "viable alternatives" to the traditional heterosexual family life style.

CHILD CARE. The *National Plan of Action* sets forth a demand that taxpayers be forced to subsidize the cost for universal child-care centers for infants, preschoolers, and school-aged children before and after school hours, in order to eliminate the necessity for women to devote any significant amount of time to mothering their own children.[12]

This proposal was designed as the response of radical feminists to the problem of the truly needy "latch-key" child who is left at home alone while both parents are out working. Instead of suggesting that social practice, economic conditions, and political policy be modified to help more mothers stay home with their children, this proposal instead mandated the federal government to set up taxpayer-financed, universally available child-care services for all families "regardless of income."

One advocate of this idea at the National Women's Conference simply stated that "parents are unnecessary" for child rearing and that children might be better raised by "trained surrogate parents" such as educators and child-care workers. By taxing the public to provide these child-care services to all families, the expressed goal was to give an economic incentive to mothers to leave the homemaking and child-caring role and instead turn to careers. The family would be automatically taxed for child-care centers, whether they used them or not, and so the incentive would be to use the child-care center and send the mother out of the home to earn extra money. The concept is to shift the primary child-care and "moral educational" function of the family during early childhood years to government-sponsored centers which would "relieve" mothers of the "burden of caring for their children."

The 1975 Ohio Task Force Report for the Implementation of the Equal Rights Amendment stated that the rationale for this kind of proposal is (1) that women must be given "equality" and "freedom" to pursue their "personal" goals, and (2) that the "sex-stereotyped attitude of society that expects mothers to care for their babies is oppressive."

The rationale given for this child-care proposal at the National Women's Conference was the following: "The equality principle embodied in the ERA requires consideration of a new public policy on the issue of child care. Women who are mothers need to enjoy the same freedoms and opportunities as men who are fathers. Mothers who desire to engage in activities outside the home, either on a full or part-time basis, must have access to child-care services so that they can fulfill their professional, educational or personal goals."[13]

Feminist political action.
THE ERA. The National Women's Conference stated this demand, in full, quite simply: "The Equal Rights Amendment should be ratified."[14] Let us say, from the outset, that this fourth proposal we are discussing does not carry the same moral weight as the other three proposals we have reviewed. The proposal on "reproductive freedom" is clearly immoral because it advocates the murder of human beings. The proposal on "sexual preference" is clearly immoral because it advocates the practice of sexual sin. The proposal on "child care" is irresponsible because it is designed to undermine the God-ordained feminine role of caring for young children. Now that we have moved on to consider the National Women's Conference's endorsement of the ERA, we are discussing an issue of political strategy rather than a direct moral issue.

Here we cannot fairly call either the "pro-ERA" or the "anti-ERA" advocates moral or immoral on the basis of their political strategy alone. Other factors must be taken into account for the Christian to decide whether or not to support this proposed amendment to the United States Constitution. We intend merely to let the reader agonize over the proper political position on the matter. Evangelical Christians are already lining up on both sides of the issue. It is an area in which there may be no direct biblical teaching to direct an automatic position.

Why is the ERA such a hotly debated issue in Christian circles as well as in society at large? As a professional psychologist, I have worked for the development of normal sexual roles in society, and thus have been actively opposed by radical feminists. But I wonder about their zealous support for the proposed Equal Rights Amendment to the U.S. Constitution.

What are the radical feminists trying to do with the ERA? How does their lobbying for the ERA fit into their other clearly immoral intentions? If the ERA were passed, would the radical feminists be able to use it somehow as leverage to achieve their agenda? Why are the radical feminists using the amendment process to the U.S. Constitution to achieve their aims? Would there be some other political strategy for insuring fair and impartial treatment of women that would be preferable to passing an amendment to the U.S. Constitution? Are we in danger of becoming unwitting participants with radical feminists who want to push their own program on the American public? These are the questions we should attempt to answer before we make up our minds whether or not to support the ERA.

The proposed Equal Rights Amendment to the Federal Constitution is worded, simply enough, that there shall be no discrimination on the basis of sex. In America's democratic form of government, there may be many different ways to insure that women are not unjustly discriminated against, including the passing of state and federal laws to that effect. The National Women's Conference endorsed the Equal Rights Amendment rather than state and federal legislation in order to forward their strategy of placing all family and domestic law under the jurisdiction of the federal courts. There is tremendous debate on what the consequences of the Equal Rights Amendment would be, but it is clearly part of the strategy of the radical feminists to move the definition of what is appropriate legal treatment of women away from state legislatures and away from the United States Congress, where we have elected representatives who can be voted in and out of office, depending upon their stance on such matters.

Section II of the ERA grants Congress specific power to enforce by "appropriate" legislation the Equal Rights Amendment, thereby potentially preempting states' rights to legislation in this area. All legislation pertaining to the sexes would become subject to review and overrule by the federal courts. All laws relating to marital duties, custody, alimony, divorce, residence, property, privacy, parental responsibility, inheritance, and so forth, would become the province of federal legislation and review, rather than the sole concern of state and local legislation and review, as is presently the case. Decisions in these areas would become less and less controllable by the general electorate. Decision-making power would be taken from the local state legislatures to be put under the bureaucratic guidelines of the federal administration under the U.S. Congress. Such power would ultimately be subject to the interpretation of the United States Supreme Court, which would have the complete and conclusive power to determine the validity of every federal or state law pertaining to the legal rights, relationships, and responsibilities of men and women.

A constitutional amendment would move the whole matter to a new arena, the federal courts, and ultimately to the United States Supreme Court, which consists of a handful of justices. These few judges would decide what the Equal Rights Amendment means, and the radical feminists are apparently satisfied that our judicial system, permeated with humanistic thought and rhetoric, will be more sympathetic to the radical feminist objectives than is the general public. It is the expressed goal of the radical feminists to remove the general electorate from directly determining matters pertaining to sex.

The radical feminists intend to use the Equal Rights Amendment, if successfully passed, to disallow all "sexist" references in all phases of our society. They will attempt to require that parents and teachers ignore the normal gender differences between the two sexes and thereby teach "unisex" concepts. They also hope to use it to advance the legal position of homosexuals in society, by eliminating the requirement that legal marriage be defined as that union involving a male and a female only. This change would allow homosexuals to ultimately marry and even adopt children. These are the stated objectives of the radical feminists in their desire to pass the Equal Rights Amendment.

We might continue to debate whether or not they can achieve these objectives through the Equal Rights Amendment, but we must admit two things: (1) The radical feminists sincerely hope to use the Equal Rights Amendment to advance their goal of destroying traditional family and marriage relationships. And (2) by adopting the strategy of passing the Equal Rights Amendment to the federal Constitution, they hope to remove the entire debate out of the legislative process where the individuals determining the rights of men and women are subject to recall or referendum. By selecting the strategy of amending the U.S. Constitution, radical feminists have only to convince a very small number of judges to be sympathetic to their cause. They will no longer need to persuade a majority of the voting public in order to advance their program. They believe their best chances lie in the arena of the federal judicial system.

The *National Plan of Action* of the National Women's Conference proposes a major cultural revolution for America.

Under the Fourteenth Amendment to the United States Constitution, women are guaranteed access to "equal protection" and "due process" through all the courts. State and federal laws have been passed in recent years to prevent discrimination against women in areas of employment, credit, education, and health care. We who are in favor of advancing the rights of women in employment, banking, and civic opportunities should propose any further *specific* legislation needed to remedy any existing inequities for women. For example, in states with unequal inheritance taxes for men and women, specific laws should be passed to correct that specific legal defect. In states where a wife cannot sue her husband for physical abuse, the law should be rewritten to provide the specific legal protection to the wife. In order to protect the special rights of women and positive discrimination in favor of women, we should continue to pass specific state and federal laws through the legislatures.

STRANGE BEDFELLOWS. In May 1979, an organization of prostitutes in the state of Florida under the name of "Coyote" made a startling announcement to the press. This "minority group" decided to ask each of its members to exercise political power by releasing to feminist action groups the names of state legislators who used prostitutes. The radical feminist groups then threatened to publicize the names of the state lawmakers who had voted against the Equal Rights Amendment, or had voted against liberalizing abortion, or had voted against bills designed to increase the political and legal power of homosexual groups.[15]

The spokeswoman for the organization of prostitutes also pointed out that the hopes of the organization for the legalization of prostitution would depend upon the passage of the Equal Rights Amendment. For this reason, the group of prostitutes was willing to threaten the state legislators who had sexual relations with them. The prostitutes threatened public exposure which would lose the legislator many votes, because of the widely held value against prostitution. In other words, the prostitutes were willing to use the public's condemnation of their own activity as a political weapon against legislators who would vote against the ERA. All along, their intention was to achieve the political goal of legalizing prostitution as a "professional" activity.

This news item clearly illustrates the close connection between the advocates of radical feminism, prostitution, homosexual advocates, and pro-abortionists. All of these movements have one thing in common: They are in revolt against marriage and the family. Activists in each of these groups are cooperating with one another to achieve their common goal of overthrowing traditional Christian standards of sexual morality. They are also unscrupulously manipulating the sensitivities of Christian morality (here expressed as outrage to promiscuous legislators) to further their attempts to overthrow that very morality.

A CRITIQUE OF RADICAL FEMINISM

It is quite possible that the agenda of the radical feminists may eventually be adopted. Why? Because the majority of people in America, although they may be against these anti-family proposals, are tragically apathetic. Another danger is the paralyzing misconception that society has no right to limit individual freedom in the public interest, the interest of other individuals, or the interest of groups such as children and the family.

Law and morality. This misconception ignores the principle established in our United States Constitution that the people have a right to regulate social behavior on moral grounds. Scripture clearly teaches that God has instituted governmental authority for the purpose of rewarding good and punishing evil (Rom. 13:1-4; 1 Peter 2:13-17). The government has the right to set limits on individual freedom in the interest of protecting the rights of other individuals or groups, or in the interest of the "common good." Government exercises its right to limit individual freedom in the cases of imprisonment, taxing income and property, and guaranteeing safety.

Assuming that the government can limit freedom of individuals, it should do so in ways that represent the will of the people as a "moral community." What moral standards should we use? That is the proper question. The American government had its roots in the moral standards of the Bible.[16] We cannot pretend that government should guarantee absolute individual rights to some groups in disregard of the moral laws of the universe.

Although the Constitution acknowledges the freedom to pursue happiness, government has always held that all freedoms are relative to other people's rights and the well-being of the general population. For example, the pursuit of happiness is regulated with limits on public expression of sexuality, limits on gambling, liquor laws, building codes, property laws, and regulations. When the individual's pursuit of happiness creates a clear and present social evil, the government may justifiably legislate against such pursuits. This has been a universally acknowledged right and duty of good government.

Society sets limits on obscenity, pornography, prostitution, homosexuality, sexual abuse of children, sexual assault, and public expressions of intimate sexuality. All of these activities could be proposed as examples of the "pursuit of happiness," but they are all examples, as well, of areas in which society has the constitutional right to set limits for the general good of the community. Society does have a right to regulate individual behavior on moral grounds and to assure a reasonable community standard of personal conduct which we call "common decency." We therefore must discriminate upon the count of sex and sexuality in these admittedly very personal areas which relate to marriage, family responsibilities, and the rearing of children according to normal heterosexual patterns.

Even though the radical feminists phrase their platform in terms of words such as "needs," "liberation," and "rights," in reality it is a superficial masquerade for the rejection of traditional moral standards of decent behavior. It is a clear rebellion against time-tested legal standards protecting social stability and structure. We have the constitutional right to determine basic social and moral codes to be enforced by our government in order to demand responsible behavior by adults. Responsible and decent behavior should be enforced by government in order to nurture our children in the most stable environment possible.

Is it a man's world? Radical feminists are not fighting for mere equal opportunity in the marketplace with men. They appear to be fighting for the opportunity to become masculine. The radical feminists believe that women in the traditional family unit suffer from carrying two "unfair" burdens: (1) the bearing of children, and (2) the responsibility for the nurture and protection of children. Their proposals are to change society's rules to make women "equal" to men by federally financing abortion on demand in any month of pregnancy so as to eliminate the first burden of bearing children. Then, through federal financing of child-care centers, they hope to eliminate the responsibility of women to nurture and raise children.

By passing the Equal Rights Amendment, they hope to be able to further obliterate any difference between the sexes by implementing their proposal for federal guaranteed freedom of sexual expression which would allow women to choose other women as marriage partners, just as men can. Many of the militant lesbians in the radical feminist groups insist that they can become equal with men only if they can have sexual relationships and marriage relationships with other women.

Unfortunately, some members of the legitimate women's rights movement, who have fought to gain the vote for women and equal pay in the marketplace, have chosen to link up with these radical feminists who want to deny their uniqueness as women altogether.

Sex is a difference. Of course, the overwhelming majority of citizens in our country are committed to providing genuinely equal opportunities for women. But, obviously, there are biological and psychological differences between men and women. We must acknowledge the difference in the female sexual identity and role as compared to the male sexual identity and role. Sex *is* a difference. It is not unfair that God made two different sexes with different rights, different privileges, and different responsibilities. Society should protect and defend these valuable differences. Woman does not equal man. And man does not equal woman.

"Equal is not synonymous with 'fair' or 'just'; nor is unequal necessarily 'unfair' or 'unjust.' Woman's vital role as homemaker clearly warrants equal opportunity but, more than that, *unequal rights, special rights,* or *protective rights* that allow her the choice to nurture and protect children in the family."[17]

Woman's rights. Should any distinction be made by society on the basis of sex? The radical feminists say no. They would challenge the normal discrimination society makes on the basis of sex in such areas as child support, military service, use of public toilets, and protecting heterosexual marriage. The radical feminists argue that we should not discriminate in favor of women to provide them unique status, in terms of economic protection for their role of nurturing and raising children in the home, free of outside employment responsibilities. They would remove the exemption of mothers of young children from military service.

Should society discriminate in favor of the pregnant woman? The radical feminists would say no. The radical feminists would remove all special rights for the woman to be financially supported and protected during pregnancy and early child rearing days. Instead, they propose "freedom" from childbearing through federally financed abortions. They propose "freedom" from child rearing responsibility by federally financed child-care centers so that women can pursue careers instead of their natural responsibilities of child rearing.

By pushing for "equal rights" the feminists are attempting to abolish the special rights of womanhood. Among these rights are certain economic and social protections afforded by marriage and the enforcement of a husband's responsibilities to protect the motherly roles of childbearing, childbirth, and child rearing.

In 1972, there was an effort to amend the national Equal Rights Amendment to recognize the special rights of the woman as wife and mother (for example, to be exempt from the draft), but all efforts to make these amendments were defeated in Congress by the active lobbying of the National Organization of Women (NOW) which is the active organization supporting the philosophy of radical feminism. It is therefore crystal clear that the agenda of the radical feminists is to remove these distinctive, positive rights of women. This special right to be a wife and a mother will be denied by the Equal Rights Amendment. This is specifically the goal of the radical feminists in sponsoring the Equal Rights Amendment. We can be sure that the radical feminists will press their case to the U.S. Supreme Court to carry out this interpretation of the ERA if it is passed, because it is clearly their purpose.

The homosexual activists and radical feminists hold the same doctrine: Treat women and men the same. To achieve this they are advocating the elimination of any and all rights, benefits, or exemptions conferred by law upon women as women, or upon men as men. Of course, at the present time most states have unequal rights and obligations imposed upon men and women: the wives' right to be financially supported and the husbands' obligation to provide the support. The radical feminists want to remove not only negative discrimination against women but positive protection as well.

Radical feminists are unfeminine. Radical feminism is actually a contradiction in terms because it denies the uniqueness of femininity. Womanhood involves a host of distinctions; among them are childbearing, nursing and caring for young children. The radical feminist not only denies these unique and unequal feminine roles, but also denies the rights of the feminine person to have these unique roles protected and preserved. The radical feminist is therefore really a *radical unisexist* who wants to obliterate the legitimate distinctions between men and women. Philosophically, morally, theologically, psychologically, and biologically, it has been traditionally recognized that it is a unique feminine role to have sexual relations with a man. But the radical feminists wish to obliterate this unique feminine attribute and to become "equal" with men by providing government sanctions and support to women who choose to have sexual relationships with other women.

The radical feminists, therefore, deny all that is uniquely feminine about women—their unequal and unique roles of childbearing, child rearing, child nursing, and child care, and being married to a man. They wish to remove these aspects of feminine identity with the sanction of U.S. federal law. In order to carry out this program of eliminating the natural childbearing consequence of normal sexual intercourse, they propose to trample down the rights of unborn humans by declaring them non-persons who can be killed with legally justified homicide. The radical feminists also pursue a deliberate plan of action designed to trample the rights of women for unique legal protection during the years of childbearing and child rearing. Extreme feminists also wish to eliminate any legal requirement that the fathers carry out their unequal responsibility to support the wife and children. In so doing, they are systematically attempting to dismember marriage and the family, all with the objective of making women "equal to men." To the radical feminists, true equality means they must have federally financed murder of their unborn children, federally financed mother substitutes for their children, and federally sanctioned rights to homosexual relationships with other women. Only then will the radical feminists feel equal to men.

Our society must ask itself whether or not it needs these kinds of equality, particularly at the price of increased taxes to murder more unborn children, to dismember the family, and to destroy normal marriage.

Family foes. As we have seen, radical feminists would deny that men have any special responsibility to support their wives and children. They transfer the responsibility for children to the shoulders of the federal government and the general taxpayer. In so doing, they are short-circuiting the family and are working to undermine the traditional family unit for raising children and for organizing society.

Radical feminists are also attempting to remove all legal limitations on the public portrayal of sexual activities of all sorts. In the past, standards of social decency have functioned to protect the stability of marriage and family relationships. But the radical feminists hope to remove all standards of acceptable public sexual conduct, relationships, and expression in front of children.

The radical feminists will not be satisfied until they have destroyed distinctions between masculine and feminine identity. They want to remove any rule that defines acceptable norms for sexual behavior as presented to children. They want to eliminate marriage as a social institution in order to guarantee "equal" rights to women. And they hope to restructure the family by removing the women's unequal burdens of carrying and caring for children.

Politics for families. Political activity is the only area in which radical feminists can achieve their program for society, and they are making major advances. They controlled millions of federal dollars to set up the National Women's Conference, thereby obtaining all the publicity that they wanted. This was accomplished by brute political maneuvering. Similarly, political activity is the major means for advocates of the traditional family unit to maintain the rights of children, the rights of marriage, and the rights of family life in our country.

We must become better informed as to the political strategies being used by radical feminists to promote their viewpoint. We must hold our public officials accountable for providing leadership representing the best interests of children and the family. We must maintain the institutions of marriage and the family, the special rights of women, and the special rights and responsibilities of men in order to maintain our moral and social order in America in the remaining years of the twentieth century.

"Politics is a branch of morals," according to Aristotle. Dr. Reed Bell has observed: "The law embodies the moral community's choice as to acceptable, normal standards of conduct. This is particularly true in relationship to children, parenting and the family."[18] The silent majority cannot remain silent much longer if we are to preserve the values of normal heterosexual family life in America.

POINT-COUNTERPOINT

Mike: George, as we look over the last chapter, it's fair to say that you gave us a serious warning against the challenge of feminist rhetoric and philosophy. It appears that what we have is one world view in conflict with another. The direction a person takes, and the conclusions he will ultimately come to, seem to be, to a great extent, dictated by the overriding philosophies he adopts at the very outset of the task.

George: Yes, I believe that the radical feminist philosophy is a special case of the humanistic world view that we were considering in chapter two.

Mike: Both the humanist and the feminist picture themselves as courageous "freedom fighters." It is quite easy, in a generation that loves a righteous struggle and admires the underdog, to be swept away in the enthusiasm of confusing conflict. Unthinking Christians, in their naive support of certain popular causes, in reality may be fighting against God. So I think it is important that we turn now from our discussion of contemporary challenges to a reexamination of the natural order and the natural limitations that the Bible says God imposes upon the created order.

George: I'd be interested if you could show how that scriptural world view has a different set of implications for our actions in the same way I tried to explain how the feminist philosophy led to a particular plan of action.

Mike: The Bible will always be calling men to come back to the fact that their social and personal actions must be explained to a God who judges all men's actions. The humanist, of course, doesn't want to consider God, and does not want to view his actions as being judged by anyone other than himself. So in a very real sense the battle fought today is not merely against the social order, but against a God who has established that social order, and against the Bible that clearly prescribes proper social and personal relationships.

FOUR
THE BATTLE AND THE BIBLE:
Critical Passages Concerning Sexual Roles

TECHNOLOGICAL LIBERATION AND MORAL SLAVERY

An amazing combination of science, administrative genius, and industry has given contemporary Western civilization a degree of freedom that is without precedent in history. In the eighteenth century, Gibbon proclaimed that one of the happiest eras of the human race fell between the accession of Augustus and the death of Aurelius (27 B.C.—A.D. 180). There is much to commend that judgment. The average Briton, for example, did not enjoy the same creature comforts as his Roman ancestors until well into the nineteenth century. Since that time however, Gibbon's judgment has been outstripped by the fantastic impact of Western technology.

Overcoming restraint. Physically at least, we have been liberated in many fundamental areas. Our "liberty" is unparalleled. In spite of the bureaucratic orchestration of our lives in this urbanized technocracy, we in the West possess the highest level of personal freedom in history. Perhaps the frontiersman was less fettered with social obligation; or the primitive less accountable to society for his actions. But in true liberation, our lot is immensely superior.

We have been liberated from labor. The average American expects the eight-hour day and the five-day week. Many put in more hours than that, but today extra hours are a sign of the "go-getter," while a century ago twelve- and fourteen-hour days would have been a matter of course.

We are substantially liberated from disease as well as labor, and in the United States we have been liberated from famine in an unprecedented manner. Although crime is a constant concern, the average American has experienced an enviable liberation from the fear of personal violence. Freedom is a reality of the twentieth century. Whether it is liberation from a shortened life span through modern medical technology, or liberation from inclement weather through indoor shopping malls (which enable us to conspicuously consume, come rain or come shine), our personal freedoms have reached new heights.

In spite of this liberation, biblically sensitive people have shown a tendency to look askance at technological progress. Likewise they have often turned a jaundiced eye upon those who protest loudly for certain kinds of moral liberation. Is it just a mindless reactionary attitude that hovers over the religious, or is there something more substantial behind this reluctance? Is there something that laughs at our efforts to be free? Is there something that frustrates our strongest desires for freedom and inevitably turns our liberty into a greater bondage than the one we escaped?

In the face of all the cries for liberation in the last quarter of the twentieth century, biblically sensitive people detect a certain uneasiness gnawing at the edges of their world view. You see, there is a tension between man's drive to be free and the biblical declaration of certain God-ordained realities. Much of our modern freedom seems to come at the expense of divine commandments. Consider the teaching of Genesis 3:16-19.

To the woman he said: "I will greatly multiply your pain in childbearing; in pain you shall bring forth children, yet your desire shall be for your husband, and he shall rule over you." And to Adam he said, "Because you have listened to the voice of your wife, and have eaten of the tree of which I commanded you, 'You shall not eat of it,' cursed is the ground because of you; in toil you shall eat of it all the days of your life; thorns and thistles it shall bring forth to you; and you shall eat the plants of the field. In the sweat of your face you shall eat bread till you return to the ground, for out of it you were taken; you are dust, and to dust you shall return."

We cannot ignore the simple fact that mankind is becoming increasingly "liberated" from the harsh facts in this passage of Scripture.

Before moving from this passage we must also consider the apostolic commentary on it by Paul in Romans 8:18-21.

I consider that the sufferings of this present time are not worth comparing with the glory that is to be revealed to us. For the creation waits with eager longing for the revealing of the sons of God; for the creation was subjected to futility, not of its own will but by the will of him who subjected it in hope; because creation itself will be set free from its bondage to decay and obtain the glorious liberty of the children of God.

Evidently much of the pain and struggle from which humanity seeks to be free is an expression of the will of God. Paul teaches us here that it is not just a matter of punishment. The fact is that the Genesis account does not necessarily teach that God's curse of the physical universe after the Fall was an edict of punishment. God brought about such a condition to instill humility in his fallen creation.

We wait with "eager longing," forced to admit the imperfection of our lives. God has programmed this imperfection into the natural world. He has done this so that men would seek perfection from God, not from themselves. God will reveal glory; God alone will bring ultimate liberation. So it seems that God sought to suppress the natural arrogance of mankind, and desired to set a constant reminder before our race, a race which is always prone to let God slip from its thoughts.

Boundless limitations. It is not enough merely to challenge the growth of knowledge and the expansion of human power over the natural order of things. For that genius which drives men to liberate themselves from the seemingly mindless tyranny of physical limitations was also instituted by God. "So God created man in his own image, in the image of God he created him; male and female he created them. And God blessed them and God said to them, 'Be fruitful and multiply, and fill the earth and subdue it; and have dominion'" (Gen. 2:27, 28).

Don't blame the devil for the new technology! It is rooted in man's basic nature to be forever expanding his influence over the physical universe. Such was the plan of God. For this task God adequately equipped man not only with sufficient mental powers but with a restless spirit.

James 4:5 speaks to the indomitable will of mankind: "The spirit which God implanted in man turns towards envious desires" (NEB). Although it is true that human nature has been infiltrated by sin, the phrase "envious desires" may refer less to the moral problem of man than to his ceaseless quest to know.[1] This quest is always hindered by sin, and God has often placed limitations upon it; but regardless, it is undeniable that this is the quest which God ordained for mankind. Man, with the image of God heavy upon him, with a fierce God-given spirit to extend himself, and with the irresistible command of God pressed upon his soul, must reach out and subdue; he must explore and understand.

God himself acknowledged the terrible potential within man: "Behold they are one people, and they have all one language; and this is only the beginning of what they will do; and nothing that they propose to do will now be impossible for them" (Gen. 11:6). Why? Because they were created in the image of God; they were given a fierce spirit to know; they were given a divine commandment which was, as are all God's commands, irresistible. They were told to subdue, rule, and understand the world. God knows man better than man knows himself.

The problem is not man's burning quest to know. The word "subdue" as a creative mandate is often misunderstood. The word in the Hebrew does not mean to conquer or to ravage, but to carefully tend and control, as a man would tend his garden. For man to draw back from knowledge would be to disobey God. He would cease to be fully man.

The problem is clear and was recorded early in our history.

The Lord saw that the wickedness of man was great in the earth, and that every imagination of the thoughts of his heart was only evil continually (Gen. 6:5).

There is the problem! As man and his achievements grow, so does his capacity to do evil. God's Word says that human iniquity will grow along with human knowledge until the time that God calls a halt to human history. Jesus said of the last days, "because wickedness is multiplied, most men's love will grow cold" (Matt. 24:12). In an intriguing description of the last days before the judgment of God, the Bible foretells that human knowledge will increase dramatically.

But you, Daniel, shut up the words, and seal the book, until the time of the end. Many shall run to and fro, and knowledge shall increase (Dan. 12:4).

So not only is man's quest for knowledge and freedom a preconditioned drive of his very nature, it is also a predetermined part of his destiny. God has ordained, ironically, both the obstacles and the energies that appear in conflict: a ceaseless drive to know and an unyielding universe.

For all the advances in technology, it is safe to insist that there has never been an era like ours in which human attainments and human misery due to sin have been so closely linked. The airplane promised freedom in time and space, but it brought destruction in war greater than we were able to imagine. Nuclear power promised unlimited energy but brings fears of poisoning the environment and destroying our civilization.

The proper response. What is to be our response to this sad fact? Men do not need to fall back from the frontiers of knowledge. They need to humble their rebellious spirits under the lordship of Jesus Christ. The Bible says that we should love God with our hearts *and* our minds. Christians too often imply that this is an either/or proposition. We need to worship God and reverence him with both our intellect and our creative powers. Our minds should not stop functioning but should be saved by the atoning power of Jesus Christ.

I am pleased to know a young man with unique scientific ability. Several years back that ability was wasted on self-indulgence and drug abuse. Then he came to Jesus Christ through the ministry of Billy Graham on television. His life was saved. He had a desire to serve God in whatever way he might be called. God called him to research, and, now that he has completed his doctoral studies, he is involved in a project that could save the lives of literally millions of people through disease control. Science has become his mission field. He is loving God with his mind. I am glad he didn't draw back from his work simply because his field of entomology is dominated by godless men who reject God's rule over the universe. Instead, he brought Christ with him. This, it seems to me, is a preeminently Christian response.

As our knowledge increases, our sense of need should also increase. It is the tragedy of our world that just the opposite occurs. Such is the blindness of our day, that we are closer to a nuclear holocaust, closer to ecological collapse, closer to social disintegration, and further from God than ever before. It is not enough to know, it is not enough to be free. Men need the Lord Jesus Christ and the power he gives against sin. Our greatest need is not to be free. Jesus said:

Come to me, all who labor and are heavy laden, and I will give you rest. Take my yoke upon you, and learn from me; for I am gentle and lowly in heart, and you will find rest for your souls. For my yoke is easy, and my burden is light (Matt. 11:28, 29).

Jesus didn't offer "liberation," he offered his lordship and his mastery over men's lives to solve the problems of their lives.

Between the lines. It is a natural human drive to overcome obstacles and seek freedom. Because of the inevitable tyranny of sin that has invaded the human heart, Christians should look very carefully at the problems that the world acknowledges and the solutions it offers. Because minds are disoriented due to sin, many problems that the world decries are really not problems at all. And many of the solutions that the world tries are worse evils than the conditions they are meant to alleviate. Those who follow Christ as Lord cannot afford to be uncritical, lest they be found, however unwittingly, in opposition to God and to his Word.

Because of this, liberation movements are not always valid for the Christian. The world so often misreads and misrepresents the real needs of men. It was not, for example, merely the black man's cry for "freedom" that should have pierced the Christian conscience. It was rather his right as a child of God to have justice from his white oppressors. God requires justice; men seem only able to make empty promises of freedom. The poor should be helped by the Christian because he has needs and God commands us to care, not because we decided that he should be liberated from an oppressive economic system.

God gives compassion; man seems able only to chant about freedom while bound in the chains of his own moral failures. Liberation and freedom become hollow slogans, a pretext to express rebellion. The truth is that there are some things from which you and I will never be free. And though our society rages against them, they will stand. Even though our world hates them, they will not change. They will stand because God has set them up.

The sexual order is one such standard. Ordained by God, it remains inviolate. The sexual role of men and women in the world is firmly fixed in nature, strongly affirmed in Scripture, and yet roundly despised in our world today. Amid all the pressure of our modern world toward a unisex mentality, one has to wonder, will the church be found affirming the truth or appeasing the world and opposing God?

Where was the church when the world revolted? As with so many liberation movements today, the women's movement was launched on some undeniable truths. Our culture *is* sexist. An unbiblical, non-Christian double standard does exist. Although Scripture clearly states in Galatians 3:28 that "there is neither male nor female; for you are all one in Christ Jesus," Christians have unfairly regarded women as inferior and often treated them condescendingly. I remember hearing a pastor in a large denominational meeting say that the woman's role "is what she should be baking in the kitchen." Not only is that a bad joke, it is an insult, and it is without biblical support. No wonder there is anger over this issue.

There is injustice here and it is undeniable that we have a wrong to be righted. But in doing so many alleged Evangelicals are taking up positions against the Word of God. A recent book by a well known "Evangelical" scholar declared that Paul, in giving command for women to be silent, was merely reflecting his pre-Christian rabbinic sentiments, and concluded that his words on the subject should be ignored.[2] Several women writers who loudly proclaim their orthodoxy insist that homosexuality is not a sin.[3] To do this they unashamedly stand in opposition to the direct statements of Scripture.

There is a great conflict brewing in the midst of Bible-believing churches today. It involves issues far more grave than are readily apparent—such as the biblical view of women in the church, and whether or not godly women are willing to accept a biblically defined role in their service for Jesus Christ. The question is equally challenging to men in the church. Will they be willing to oppose their cultural prejudices when such prejudice is clearly refuted by God's Word? The outcome of this question is in considerable doubt and the impact of our decisions on the matter will have repercussions in a multitude of areas in our lives.

A DIFFICULT PASSAGE—1 TIMOTHY 2

The Bible is clear in teaching that wives are to be submissive to their own husbands. It is equally clear that a woman should not teach a man in the church. It is all too easy to accommodate the logic of the world and force the Scriptures into a straitjacket of contemporary thinking. All of us are tempted at times to make Scripture mean what we want it to mean. We are all too often ready to make interpretations of God's Word that satisfy our particular predisposition on a given matter. One particular danger in this "contemporizing" exegesis is that today's innovation becomes tomorrow's passe doctrine. God's truth, however, is eternal.

Before the clamor of woman's liberation, the Scripture was always seen as restricting the woman's role as a teacher in the church. It does little good to refute this general posture of the church by finding isolated historical instances when some small bands of poorly educated people allowed women to take preeminent preaching roles in direct opposition to Scripture. The fact that God blessed in any way is more a testimony to his grace than to his appreciation of their liberal attitudes. They were more untaught than liberal, more pragmatic than doctrinally precise.

Why has the church been so consistent in its view that Scripture restricts women in the teaching ministry? Is it because of unqualified male chauvinism? This is an important question to answer. What is the reason behind the prohibitions of Scripture concerning who and who will not teach men in Christian assemblies?

One of the most controversial texts in the debate is 1 Timothy 2:8-15.

I desire then that in every place the men should pray, lifting holy hands without anger or quarreling; also that women should adorn themselves modestly and sensibly in seemly apparel, not with braided hair or gold or pearls or costly attire but by good deeds, as befits women who profess religion. Let a woman learn in silence with all submissiveness. I permit no woman to teach or to have authority over men; she is to keep silent. For Adam was formed first, then Eve; and Adam was not deceived, but the woman was deceived and became a transgressor. Yet the woman will be saved through bearing children, if she continues in faith and love and holiness, with modesty.

When trying to understand this particular passage, it is of the utmost importance that we let ourselves be reminded by the context of the entire letter. The above instructions were intended for implementation in the local church.

I hope to come to you soon, but I am writing these instructions to you so that, if I am delayed, you may know how one ought to behave in the household of God, which is the church of the living God, the pillar and bulwark of the truth (1 Tim. 3:14, 15).

Beyond the consideration of any one issue, it is a much neglected New Testament truth that doctrinal matters should be the first and foremost concern, not of the theological seminary, nor of the academic world, *but of the local church.* It is the local church that is to be "the pillar and bulwark of the truth." Equipped by the Spirit with gifted men as elders, deacons, and pastor-teachers, the church is to come to grips with doctrinal issues within a crucible of responsibility that only personal and prolonged ministry provides.

It is a grave mistake to leave the task of theological thinking and discussion solely in the hands of the seminaries, while the local church wanders down a road of "professionalism" and gimmickry, amid an ever-expanding assortment of discarded methods and yesterday's "strategies." The problem, seldom stated, is this: If unchecked, the academic freedom, demanded by the classroom, at times can undermine a Christian's sense of responsibility to the truth, not to mention his responsibility to people whose lives are built on that truth. A local church can provide that sense of accountability which is so easily lost in the necessary "freedom" of the classroom. The local church must take its place alongside the seminary in the definition and articulation of theology.

Certainly a balance must be struck. Unfortunately, several generations of "professional clergymen" espousing pragmatic methodologies, geared to reach the broadest spectrum of interest possible, have left many of our country's pulpits in a morass of banality. As a consequence, the general public's respect for the pulpit as a place for a reasonable presentation of logical truth is in serious decline. To be sure, the pulpit is held in contempt among many thinking people; even, sadly enough, among a number of Christians.

When banality in the pulpit is backed by the insistence that the seminary, not the local church, is the place for serious theological thought, the end result is an almost total loss of authoritative instruction by the church. A serious challenge faces us within this vicious circle. Seminaries all too quickly lose accountability while local churches all too quickly lose credibility.

Prayer and the "Y" chromosome. Verse 8 of 1 Timothy 2 encourages men to pray. The word which Paul uses is *anér*, a Greek word which is used here with the definite article, strongly implying the male sex.[4] Paul earlier used the generic *anthropos* (v. 1) and it is clear that there he refers to both men and women under the generic title "men." Here the use of *anér* indicates that he is focusing on the duties in worship incumbent on the male. Men are to take a lead in prayer. They are, according to verse 8, to avoid the masculine pitfalls of anger and competitive strife that so easily mar masculine fellowship. Of course, Paul is not prohibiting women from praying; his command in verse 1 seems general enough in that regard. Here he seems to talk about male responsibility in the matters of prayer, saying in essence, "Men, don't grieve the Spirit when you pray by exhibiting those typically masculine weaknesses of temper and conflict. Don't indulge your Y chromosomes."

Ego-tripping your weaker brother. With verse 9 Paul moves from a brief remark concerning male responsibility to a more elaborate discussion of the woman's role in the local church. His first observation is that women have a definite responsibility in their dress habits. This is based on the obvious reality that sexual arousal in the male is much more quickly stimulated through eye contact, and the woman should treat the man as a "weaker brother" in this area. Sexual arousal through visual stimulation is fine when the eye is fixed on one's wife. Jesus made it very clear that any other stimulation is as bad as adultery in God's sight. The Scriptures recognize the peculiar vulnerability of many men in this area, and so Paul counsels women to accept the responsibility of appropriate dress.

This is very difficult in a society that has come to accept the propriety of women dressing for every occasion with the intention of "turning heads" and appearing seductive. Many women today uncritically wear, even to public worship, clothing that would have been considered the attire of a prostitute fifty years ago.

Such dress is not only a problem in the "eye of the beholder." It is mainly a "problem" in the mechanics of sexual arousal, and women must accept responsibility in this. It is conceivable, should style continue in its present deplorable trend, that Christian women will have to accept the fact that they will be hopelessly out of style.

SETTING THE PACE. There is a male responsibility in this matter that would greatly help the woman obey Scripture's command. Men must begin to show their appreciation for modest dress. They should give more attention than they do to the woman who dresses properly. This would be particularly true of single men in the church. A great deal of support could be shown to the woman who is being responsible in this area; support can range from compliments to dinner engagements.

The married man should be sensitive in his support of his wife's and his daughter's attire. The wife should not be encouraged to dress to boost his male ego. Likewise his concern for the attractive yet modest appearance of his daughter will be more appreciated by that daughter than most fathers realize. This is particularly true if the father approaches the matter more as a friend than as a censor. Admittedly, this concern is better received when it is first shown early in the father-daughter relationship. A heavy-handed intrusion into a teenager's dress habits after years of seeming indifference is rightly resented.

THE PLASTIC CHURCH. Has the local church been invaded by the world? Our society appeals to vanity through the constant pressure to be stylish and through inordinate emphasis on physical appearance. The more the church parrots the world, the more this becomes true of our attitudes. As the church becomes increasingly involved with contemporary visual media, the emphasis on physical attractiveness becomes even more of an issue. In the whole matter of vanity, style, and physical appearance, it is time the church began to use a little more critical judgment and stopped allowing the Tonight Show to set the pace for the way God's people present themselves to the world.

It is interesting, however, that Paul, in 1 Timothy 2, does not set down rigid guidelines. Cultures change, people are different in appearance and in response. Consequently, what is needed are not rules which could quickly become outmoded, but rather principles which should be given constant attention. We are called to be modest and to make that a constant concern in the midst of changing standards in a jaded world. We should put away the tape measures for checking hemlines and simply begin to ask ourselves, "Why am I dressing this way?" "Am I wearing this to attract attention and admiration?" "Am I dieting or exercising for the sake of my health or my vanity?" If believers spent as much time adorning their lives with "good deeds" as they do adorning their bodies with costly clothing, their walk with God would be far more effective.

Is silence golden? In verses 11-14 the controversial matter of the silence of women in the local church is raised. Paul says a woman is to "learn in silence with all submissiveness." The Greek word that Paul uses here for "silence" does not mean being mute. It means "quietness."[5] *Hesuchia* is used of both man and woman in verse 2 of the same chapter. It is a different word than is employed by Paul in 1 Corinthians 14:34 where, respecting the prophetic or didactic gifts, Paul instructs women not to say a word. The word *hesuchia*, used in 1 Timothy, does not restrict sharing or praying per se; it merely calls women to a quiet spirit, to avoid contention in the instructional ministry of the local church.

The sum total of this silent submissiveness is amplified clearly in verse 12. It is clear from this verse that women are prohibited from "teaching" or having "authority over men" in the local church. The word "teach" is fairly clear, but what does Paul mean when he forbids women to "have authority over men"? The verb Paul uses, *authentein*, meant originally, in a literal sense, "to be an independent actor."[6] It seems best to see this as discouraging women from taking a public leadership position regarding the instruction of men in the local church.[7] With added emphasis, Paul closes verse 12 by repeating himself. "She is to keep silent."

PUNISHMENT, PREJUDICE OR PRINCIPLE? Paul offers his own reasons for this in the cryptic message of verses 13, 14. To understand Paul's remarks, we must first reject the initial impression that woman's silent and submissive role, as touching instruction in the local church, is enjoined as a punishment. Paul is not saying that women were given this position because Eve "blew it" in the Garden of Eden, and God has had it in for women ever since. No! Paul, in good rabbinic form, is going back to the creation story in order to draw upon principles of proper leadership that are expressed in human sexuality. Adam was formed first, then Eve. Whose plan was that? Was this merely an arbitrary order of events? No, God does not act arbitrarily. God didn't flip a cosmic coin in eternity and say, "Heads, I'll make man first." There was a plan to it. And when, under the pressure of satanic assault, that order of leadership was reversed and Eve initiated action, the result was catastrophic. Paul is saying, in so many words, "Haven't you learned that lesson yet?"

It is no wonder that Satan assaulted Eve first; she was a woman, made by God to be ever so sensitive to spiritual input. She was made to respond, and Satan lured her to take independent initiative. Women are not to be leaders in the church because God has not decreed that function for the female. This is not owing to a deficiency of judgment, or of intellect; rather, primary leadership would be a misuse of the beautiful function of supportive response that God has worked into female sexuality.

THE UNAVAILABLE MALE. Transgression is inevitable when men fail in their spiritual responsibility to lead, and women rush to assume a role God never intended them to exercise. This is still a constant concern today as it was in Paul's day and as it was in the garden. The prime rationale for women usurping authority over men in the church is that "if there is no man to do it, then a woman will." This is wrong. May God give us the courage to say that if there is no man to do it, then it will not be done *at that time*. This is a biblical principle.

When Paul journeyed to Philippi (Acts 16:11, ff.) there was no synagogue. So he went immediately to the bank of a river. Why? In Jewish tradition if there were not ten men (a *minyan*), public prayer and teaching could not be held in a synagogue. Those who desired prayer and worship were to find a ceremonially clean place to meet and there ask God to provide leadership. That was why Acts 16 tells us that Paul and Luke "supposed there was a place of prayer" by a river (16:13). A riverside was a ceremonially clean place. Lacking male leadership, women met to worship and pray and Paul "sat down and spoke to the women who had come together" (v.13). Before Paul took leave of Philippi, God had prospered the work and male leadership was raised up. Luke evidently remained to continue discipleship work, and as Paul's letter to the Philippians indicates, the church grew, grounded on the work of many godly women (Phil. 4:2), but ultimately blessed with responsible male leadership (Phil. 1:1).

We reverse the created order at great peril. The created sexual order suggests that in matters of spiritual leadership, the man should move out first. Women should not be taking the lead or assuming the authority that is inherent in the act of teaching men. More will be said about what is communicated within human sexuality, but we should once more insist that these instructions of Paul, as 1 Timothy 3:14, 15 clearly points out, were to be applied only to the church. The local church, not the public classroom or the university hall, is the focus here. In the church, a woman's silent submissiveness gives almost sacramental affirmation of the rule of God and the Lordship of Christ. It is an acknowledgment of God's sovereign right to govern his people.

An inconceivable interpretation. Verse 15 of chapter 2 is open to many curious interpretations. One thing we must reject is the initial impression of a sort of "conceptual regeneration." We know from an avalanche of Scripture that all persons are saved by faith in the atoning work of the Lord Jesus. In this context the word "saved" must have its broader idea of "preserved" or "given full expression and meaning." The verb translated "childbearing" has been understood in various ways. The obvious meaning of pregnancy must be considered, but some have noted the appearance of a definite article and suggest that it refers to "the childbearing," e.g., the bearing of Christ by the virgin Mary.[8] Another possibility is that it is used in a figurative sense of "femininity."[9] If that is possible, Paul would be saying here that women will find their deepest sense of fulfillment in accentuating their femininity and continuing to reproduce the fruits of the Holy Spirit, here listed as faith, love, and holiness with modesty.

IN THE BEGINNING

Since Paul draws his theological arguments from the book of Genesis, let's consider next that formative passage on sexual roles found in Genesis 1: 27, 28.

So God created man in his own image, in the image of God he created him; male and female he created them. And God blessed them, and God said to them, "Be fruitful and multiply, and fill the earth and subdue it; and have dominion over the fish of the sea and over . . . the earth."

There can be absolutely no question that the essential equality of the sexes is a clear teaching of this fundamental passage concerning human sexuality. One sex was not considered "more" in the image of God than another. Mankind was created "in the image of God." Whatever that means, and there is considerable debate as to what it means,[10] all agree that it is a unique feature of the human race and that it is equally applicable to either sex. The image of God is part of what makes us human. It is also that which relates us in a special way to God, the Creator of all things.

THE GREAT NEUTER BEING IN THE SKY. The whole question of sexuality and its relation to the Godhead is an intriguing one. Is it wrong to attribute sexuality to God as well as to man? Scripture repeatedly uses the human sexual relationship to clarify and instruct concerning the nature, not only of man's relationship to God, but also of the relationship within the Trinity itself. It seems to be a great mystery, but the fact is that Scripture suggests the sexuality of God. It is wrong to conceive of God as "that great neuter Being in the sky." Everything that modern psychologists, biologists, and anthropologists are discovering about human sexuality—its creative power, its force in defining our personality, its contribution to so much that is meaningful in our life—can be appreciated within the Godhead as well.

The man upstairs. To deepen the mystery while still affirming the sexuality of God, we note that the Scriptures ascribe the attributes of both sexes to God. Male characteristics are seen in the many references to God as both Father and Son. His manly attributes are declared in his many roles as Warrior or Kinsman Redeemer. And, contrary to much current opinion, there is undeniable significance in the constant reference to God, Father, Son, and Holy Spirit, by the masculine qualifiers such as pronouns and adjectives. The popular joke, "Tell it to God, she'll understand," is funny but it is not biblical.

She'll understand. Nonetheless, God displays the attributes of a female as well as a male. Without hesitation Isaiah compares the God of Israel to a compassionate mother (Isa. 66:13). Jesus speaks of his concern for Jerusalem and compares himself to a "mother hen" (Matt. 23:37). The Holy Spirit, though often referred to by male pronouns and adjectives, is often portrayed as displaying attributes that seem most feminine. This can be noted from the Spirit's very first appearance in Genesis, brooding over the creation in an almost maternal sense.[11] From the outset, what God the Father plans and God the Son executes, God the Spirit nurtures with a sensitivity that is undeniably feminine. Though all its implications may be shrouded in mystery, it seems a great mistake to deny or even ignore the sexuality of God as it is expressed in passionate care, creative power, and constant nurture.

LOSING THE PICTURE—ROMANS 1

Once again we are driven to the inescapable conclusion of the Bible that human sexual behavior is inextricably woven together with truth about God. It is worthwhile to repeat what was stated earlier, namely, that a tampering with the sexual order can result in great confusion over the nature of God. Romans 1 makes it undeniable that there is a connection, an interacting connection, that exists between proper human sexual expression and proper human perception of the nature and requirements of God.

For what can be known about God is plain to them, because God has shown it to them. . . . Therefore God gave them up in the lusts of their hearts to impurity, to the dishonoring of their bodies among themselves, because they exchanged the truth about God for a lie and worshiped and served the creature rather than the Creator, who is blessed forever! Amen. For this reason God gave them up to dishonorable passions. Their women exchanged natural relations for unnatural, and the men likewise gave up natural relations with women and were consumed with passion for one another, men committing shameless acts with men and receiving in their own persons the due penalty for their error. And since they did not see fit to acknowledge God, God gave them up to a base mind and to improper conduct (Rom. 1:19, 24-28).

When a man or a woman fails in sexual responsibilities, he or she no longer reflects truth about God through sexual behavior. With the loss of that natural aspect of revealing God's nature comes a spiraling increase within a society of idolatry in all its subtleties. With the loss of "truth about God," sexual confusion accelerates and expands. The end result is a society that is "foolish, faithless, heartless, ruthless. Though they know God's decree that those who do such things deserve to die, they not only do them but approve those who practice them" (Rom. 1:31, 32). In short, to reject God's concern for human sexual behavior produces, initially, moral impotence, and ultimately, irremedial perversion of the worst kind.

Going to school. There is truth about God "wrapped up" in women behaving like women and men behaving like men. That is why sexual roles are to be attended to with precision in the church and the home according to biblical teaching. The church and home are the two great schools of theology that God has established for the basic instruction of mankind about himself. The church and the home are to care about sexual roles because truth about God is at stake.

Convention or crisis? There is unique truth about God in masculinity and there is unique truth about God in femininity. If we surrender to a unisex mentality we will lose a great teaching device that God has built into the universe. The church and home are to underwrite this truth that God has wrapped up in human sexuality. This is the logic behind Paul's remarks. He is reflecting his theological concerns, not his sociological conditioning. Women are equal with men; Paul knew that, of course. But as there is functional subordination within the Trinity, so there is to be a functional subordination within the sexual order. Women, when they adopt a submissive restraint within the church and refuse to instruct men, are, in fact, protecting eternal truth about God. Romans 1:24 warns us that the man or woman who ignores this is in jeopardy.

Though it was not the original purpose of the women's movement, endorsement of homosexuality is becoming increasingly an issue in the ranks. The reason for this is obvious. As people, even God's people, male or female, back off from sexual responsibility, homosexuality is seen as an acceptable alternative. Disobedience and rebellion are becoming more and more of a problem. As a result, our society, our churches, and, tragically, even our own children may grow resistant to the gospel's call to repentance and faith.

AN EVEN MORE DIFFICULT PASSAGE— 1 CORINTHIANS 11

There is a grave issue at stake within the Christian home and the Christian church concerning sexual roles and sexual order. If

women do not behave as women and men do not behave as men
in their responsibilities before God, Evangelical Christianity will
reap a whirlwind. There is more at stake than domestic
tranquility, or bourgeois efficiency within the middle class. The
issue is, do we honor God and do we obey his Word? The
consequences are greater than just our peace of mind. If we
honor God we will save ourselves and our children. If we do not
we will lose far more than our middle class mores.

Look once more at 1 Corinthians 11:2-16.

*I commend you because you remember me in everything and
maintain the traditions even as I have delivered them to you. But
I want you to understand that the head of every man is Christ,
the head of a woman is her husband, and the head of Christ is
God. Any man who prays or prophesies with his head covered
dishonors his head, but any woman who prays or prophesies with
her head unveiled dishonors her head—it is the same as if her
head were shaven. For if a woman will not veil herself, then she
should cut off her hair; but if it is disgraceful for a woman to be
shorn or shaven, let her wear a veil. For a man ought not to
cover his head, since he is the image and glory of God; but
woman is the glory of man. (For man was not made from
woman, but woman from man. Neither was man created for
woman, but woman for man.) That is why a woman ought to
have a veil on her head, because of the angels. (Nevertheless, in
the Lord woman is not independent of man nor man of woman;
for as woman was made from man, so man is now born of
woman. And all things are from God.) Judge for yourselves; is it
proper for a woman to pray to God with her head uncovered?
Does not nature itself teach you that for a man to wear long hair
is degrading to him, but if a woman has long hair, it is her pride?
For her hair is given to her for a covering. If any one is disposed
to be contentious, we recognize no other practice, nor do the
churches of God.*

This passage is best set forward with the understanding that it
regulates, not the worship service of the church, but the home
worship. This would help relieve the apparent contradiction
between 1 Corinthians 11:5 and 14:34. Paul begins instruction on

church assemblies appropriately enough with his remarks on communion in 1 Corinthians 11:17.

Veils and submission. Initially in this passage we are impressed by the merging of physical roles of man and wife and the heavenly roles of the Father and the Son. Though there is considerable discussion and disagreement on the wearing of veils, that issue is not the focus of this study. It is true, however, that if this is a regulation concerning family worship, then the whole question concerning veils is somewhat reduced.

It is clear that non-eternal, clearly cultural matters penetrate this passage. To acknowledge this, however, is not to say that their inclusion detracts at all from the inspiration or authority of this entire account. But certainly Paul intended some of his remarks to have bearing only on the church at Corinth. For example, he was not unaware of the diverse practices in the Old Testament, such as the taking of Nazarite vows, which included growing long hair, when he wrote that "nature" itself taught that long hair was degrading to a man. Paul certainly intended the word "nature" to refer only to the cultural context of Corinth, not to the entire world of men, of whose pluralistic mores Paul had some firsthand experience. The problem is, as always, how does one extricate the eternal from the cultural? Basically, our work should not do violence to the context of the passage and the broader context of collaborating biblical evidence found elsewhere in Scripture. If the New Testament had several references to the mandatory wearing of veils we would be much more reluctant to dismiss the passage as merely reflecting cultural conditioning. The fact is, it does not.

In 1 Corinthians 11:3 Paul speaks of three relationships. Two are invisible: the relationship between man and God and between the Father and the Son. One is visible: the relationship between man and wife. Subordination is called for in each relationship: man to God, Son to Father, and wife to husband. As the wife is submissive to her husband, she is a picture of Jesus Christ. In her submissiveness the wife declares and praises the sovereign power and rightful Lordship of God the Father. A woman no more loses equality in her submission than Christ loses deity. This is a matter of function, not of essence.

The woman, in being submissive, becomes a picture of spiritual truth. As man submits to God, so a wife submits to her husband. This is a loving, trusting non-manipulative act of the will. Verse 7 tells us that the man in his role as male is "the image and glory of God." That is, he manifests in his role certain truth about God. The word "glory" often means the manifest presence of God.[12] The verse goes on to say that a woman is "the glory of man." Though it is obscure, verse 7 seems to indicate that woman, in her female role, portrays the pinnacle of humanity. The woman expresses, in her femininity, the highest qualities of being human. As Ephesians 5 boldly teaches, the submissive wife and mother is a picture, a role model, of the believer.

Thus endeth civilization. Although women have not taken the lead in the production of art in most civilizations, nonetheless, any culture which has been responsive to the woman's sensitivity, which has honored woman's place and given respect to the woman's role in life, has always produced the most humane, refined, and civilized society. A male chauvinist culture is a dreary subhuman mess. A good illustration of this would be a cartoon I once saw. It pictured a gross, pot-bellied, beer-drinking, cigar-smoking husband, sitting, semi-comatose, in the midst of countless empty beer cans. As he sits, bleary-eyed in his under-shirt before the TV, watching yet another football or baseball game, his wife, suitcase in hand, strides toward the door shouting back: "Thus ends civilization as you know it." The woman is the glory of the man.

SOLVING A MYSTERY

Though Ephesians 5:24 tells us that it is a "great mystery," the wife is a picture of the believer; and the husband, a picture of Christ. The woman prefigures the believer, not just in her piety to God, but in her submission to her husband. No matter how proficient she may be in prayer, regardless of the wealth of her biblical knowledge, if she does not learn submission to her husband, the wife will fail to communicate to her children the necessary role modeling they will need to better follow Christ. Just as the man, through his role as husband, embodies the authority of Christ, so the woman, in her submissive behavior, pictures the proper response to Christ's authority. The generation of believers that does not encourage the woman to accept her God-appointed role in church and home will produce a generation of children who will not serve Christ.

The husband has a burden to lovingly picture the dignity and authority of the Lord Jesus. The wife has the burden to lovingly picture the proper response to Jesus' right to be Lord of all. As the woman submits, as she fulfills all those things in Scripture that many portray as repressive, she is liberated. She becomes a master teacher in the two greatest of schools, the church and the home. Her best pupils are those she loves the most. The education that she can give through accepting her submissive role is of inestimable worth in an age when men's hearts are failing because of fear, faithlessness, and unbelief.

The church or home that ignores the role of women according to Scripture deprives its children of effective models for believing behavior. Without submissive women and loving male leadership, our bearings are lost. A husband can survive an unsubmissive wife. Often he adjusts by working late, and on weekends. Or he plays a lot of golf. But can the children survive? A church can grow with women in places of spiritual leadership, but will its children be nurtured and survive?

Throwing out the first stone. If blame must be placed on anyone concerning the confusion over the role of women in the church and home, then it should be placed on the man. Men in America have neglected to honor the woman in her role as Jesus honored her. Condescending and demeaning language about women have no place in the vocabulary of a Christian man. Yet, always in humorous asides, one can hear in almost every church phrases like "my old lady" or "my ball and chain" or "the little woman." This shouldn't be too surprising, since it is only recently that racially discriminative phrases have left our pulpit vocabularies.

Rabbis and playboys. Unfortunately, our male-dominated society has continued to exploit women sexually. One wonders how much male chauvinism in the church is a result of Paul's so-called rabbinic bias, and how much is a product of the pompous ponderings of Hugh Hefner. I believe God will hold the man most responsible. It is often the man who pressures the woman out of the home and into the job market. Object: new car, new boat. Casualties: functional orphans, except for the hours between 5:30 P.M. and bedtime. It is the man who so often demands the abortion. Over the past two years my wife and I have worked with an organization that encourages unwed mothers to consider alternatives to abortion. We have been dismayed to discover how many young girls wanted to keep their babies, but an angry boyfriend or an embarrassed father threatened to disown them and deprive them of love at their most vulnerable hour unless they took the life of their child. Like it or not, in our church and in our world, it is the man who stands most guilty in the failure to assume his God-given sexual responsibilities.

Getting off the dime. It is high time the church started acknowledging the great power and importance there is in being a woman. The church has failed, and consequently it is vulnerable to the attacks of Satan in this area. When a misguided feminist challenges the supposed sexism of the New Testament, Evangelical apologists rush to the defense, but often expose their own male chauvinism. "The New Testament is not sexist," they cry. "A woman can do everything a man can." Well, that is not true. It is not true psychologically, biologically, or theologically. And the reverse is just as clear: A man cannot do everything a woman can. There is nothing demeaning in this difference.

It is time for the church to magnify the woman's role. She needs no male emancipation proclamation, for Christ has set her free. The church must acknowledge this fact and continue to affirm that the home and the church are the two great God-ordained institutions to teach moral truth about God and man. In those two places the woman, the great picture of a believer, is to be submissive to male leadership and not teach or take authority.

This restriction is not commanded by Scripture in any other area of life. She is not limited in commerce, in secular education, nor in politics. Wives are to be submissive to their own husbands and women are not to teach men in the church. These restrictions and duties are not in force in any other institution. They are in force in the church and the home in order to condition the proper reverence and humble attitudes that all of us are to adopt before God. They are in force in the church and the home in order to continue to communicate truth about God as male and female. They are in force to reflect God's gentle nurture and to help us honor his sovereign leadership. Sexual distinctions in leadership are in force in the church and in the home in order to *reverse* the rejection of human sexuality that sin always engenders.

Satan isn't sexy. The devil hates sex. He wants to cheapen it, level it, and make it boring. Consequently, he inflates its importance in our culture outside the boundaries of God's protective guidelines. Having made sex a matter of compulsive-obsessive neurosis in our world, Satan proceeds to bring men into its bondage through fear and perversion. His goal is human impotence, both morally, creatively, and physically. The sad testimony of modern literature, TV, music, and art bears mute witness to how successful he has been. A society that refuses to accept the sexual roles that God sets forth will create a climate of indifference to the commands of God to love and serve him. It will create a climate of indifference about our responsibility to others in tenderness and compassion. A denial of proper sexual roles is ultimately a denial of God and man.

There are great issues pressing upon Evangelicals, challenging our ability both to hold and to articulate God's plan concerning sexual distinctions and differences. If we fail to accept the Word of God, God's people, along with the world, will be swept away in the coming maelstrom of homosexuality and rebellion. Such rebellion stands ready to break upon our country like an angry wave. It is a rebellion against any authority, against the Word of God, against the Lordship of Christ, and ultimately, a rebellion against the gospel itself. May God give us the courage to hold to Scripture in the shadow of this tidal wave, though the world hate us for it.

SECTION TWO

THE
CONFLICT
BETWEEN
US

INTRODUCTION
THE STATE OF OUR UNIONS

Mike: I think the titles for our sections tip our hand. We see that the sexual revolt going on around us has produced a great deal of sexual confusion within us. It is almost inevitable that that confusion within us is going to spill over into serious conflict. George, I don't know if you have found in your work as a Christian psychologist the same things I have found as a pastor. But I am being overwhelmed at the problems facing the marriage relationship today. Our society abounds with serious examples of failure to successfully pull off this thing called "marriage."

George: When people come to see me for marriage counseling, I repeatedly find a tremendous amount of confusion that's been brought about by those word games we were talking about in the second chapter. A lot of people don't know if pornography is right or wrong, or if extramarital relationships are right or wrong, or if any of these things constitute a serious threat to their marriages. As a result of this confusion, they have no consistent standards for their behavior. As they get involved in some of these things, they get caught up in their consequences. Certainly, this moral confusion is at the root of their marital conflicts. So I have to agree with you, Mike, that this kind of confusion leads directly to problems of conflict in a person's sexual life.

Mike: Someone may hear you say that and all too quickly dismiss the observation as something that is true in the secular

world but certainly not true among Christians. I'm afraid,
however, that this confusion is even rampant among believers.
Word games and the confusion that they produce fall heavily
upon the Christian community. It seems to me that the Christian
community is losing contact with its biblical moorings. It is no
longer succeeding, biblically, in defending godly behavior in terms
of true sexuality and the relationships between men and women.
The Christian community is losing a biblical understanding under
this secular wave of new terms and new thoughts. Actually, it's
age-old, it's the same old pattern of immoral behavior, but it is
justified now by a very sophisticated rhetoric. And I thought that
your chapter on the issue really revealed the deadly confusion
which comes from the deliberate deception fostered by many
sexual liberation advocates. It does a great deal to help explain
why 40 percent of all marriages today end in divorce, and many
more of the marriages that don't end in divorce are really
marriages lived "in quiet desperation."

George: In my counseling with many of those who suffer from
the results of broken homes, broken marriages, or immoral
sexual experimentation, I see an obvious tendency today for
people to seek after self-fulfillment and self-gratification in their
quest to get all they can out of life for themselves. This in
contrast to those biblical principles that you were setting forth in
chapters one and four concerning submission to God's will in
these matters.

Mike: The self-assertive seventies have really almost obscured these
principles, haven't they? We have long held that personal happiness
and personal fulfillment lie in giving ourselves to causes and issues
that are greater than ourselves. But today we are so self-sensitive and
so hungry for self-fulfillment that we may be deceiving ourselves and
actually digging ourselves deeper into frustration. Actually, this
misdirection often ironically results in a decline in personal fulfillment.

George: You know, so often people who come to me ask these
kinds of questions: "How can I be more fulfilled? How can you
help me to get more out of my sex life? How can you help me to
achieve greater levels of self-fulfillment and self-gratification?"
Sometimes I think that members of the psychological profession

have actually contributed to the delinquency of people in that regard because we have so heavily emphasized self-actualization and self-fulfillment. People are coming with that question on their mind. Sometimes I wonder, as a Christian, if these people are coming to me with the wrong question. They recognize conflicts, but then they ask the wrong questions. They seek more self-fulfillment, but only in a kind of humanistic framework in which they themselves remain autonomous individuals. Self-fulfillment becomes a synonym for self-centeredness.

Mike: The pursuit of self-fulfillment becomes a dead-end street, doesn't it? It has much promise to it, but nothing to deliver. Isn't it strange, how the words of Jesus find contemporary vindication: "He who would gain his life must lose it"? Jesus invites us to make an investment in him and in God and in his Word, trusting that our commitment to someone greater than ourselves will produce the maximum happiness. Christ asks us to submit our wills to the will of God. Perhaps that's why we should first map out the whole issue of submission in its broadest doctrinal expression in the Scriptures. I had a little bit of reservation about discussing the biblical doctrine of submission in the section dealing with marriage—because submission goes far beyond the issues of marriage. And yet I don't think we can successfully cope with the problems that face marriage today without a sound understanding of the biblical doctrine of submission. Unfortunately, so often submission is talked about only in terms of the marriage relationship, and even then, only in terms of female duty. I hope that in our chapter that follows we'll see that the biblical doctrine of submission is a holistic one. Hopefully, it will help us cope with the confusion within us that breeds these conflicts.

George: I'm afraid we are going to see a stark contrast between that *concept* of submission which we find in Scripture and the practice of many modern marriages. Self-sacrifice is almost an archaic and naive concept to the modern mind. It is looked down upon by people who are perhaps more concerned about weighing what they're putting into marriage against what they're getting out of the marriage. The Christian concepts of submission and fidelity in marriage are almost laughable to modern man. They seem so hopelessly unattainable and perhaps downright naive.

Mike: They're laughing all the way to their therapists, aren't they, George?

George: Well, perhaps our profession wouldn't be so lucrative if people followed biblical teaching on marriage. In any event, I think we are going to see that our discussion on submission and the description of modern marriage will be in stark contrast with one another. But actually, it will set forth for the reader the clear choices in the matter. We can either go along with the stream, be conformed to this world, follow after the vain thinking of the humanists on marriage, or we can choose to submit to God's plan for marriage. These two chapters will look very different, but our intention is to set forth the irreconcilable difference between modern-day misdirections and the ageless truth of God's revealed will.

FIVE
A REMEDY FOR REBELLION:
The Biblical View of Submission

THE COST OF COMMUNICATION

Someone once said that "communication is costly." Those of us who labor in the field of communication will readily agree to this. It seems to be one of Mr. Jefferson's "self-evident" truths. Perhaps the greatest barrier to communication is the fact that it involves words. Words can be tricky and elusive. And it's clear that the accurate use of language is becoming a lost art; it is being replaced by popular jargon.

If communication is costly, that probably explains why most newspapers cost only fifteen cents. You see, a good number of words are being thrown around today, but very little is being said.

All of this tends to make us very suspicious of language, and of those who use it. Americans admire men such as Count von Moltke, a learned Prussian soldier of whom it was said, "He knows how to be silent in nine different languages." Give us men of action—strong, silent types. Give us men like Gary Cooper whose cool blue eyes (they were blue, weren't they?) rivet us while all he says is "yup" or "nope." We admire that. After all, didn't Jesus say, "Let your 'yups' be 'yups' and your 'nopes' be 'nopes'"? (Matt. 5:37, paraphrased). Too many words confuse us and we just don't trust them. Shaw said it all too well in *Pygmalion:* "The English have no respect for their language and will not teach their children to speak it."

Perhaps the problem is that most of the words with which you and I wrestle are in the English language. At times English can be as slippery as a hooked fish. What would it be like trying to learn English as a second language? No wonder so many third world countries dislike us. It's not our imperialism, it's our language. American idioms defy all reason. How would you translate, "I want to lay something heavy on ya" into Arabic? How do you explain to someone from Kuwait that "slim chance" and "fat chance" mean the same thing?

However, there is one particular idiom afoot today that has a good deal of biblical potential. It comes from the world of show business and it goes, "Get your act together." It is a good phrase and usually describes the act of ordering your life, aligning your priorities, realizing your resolutions, putting your house in order, and doing the constructive and proper thing. In short it means . . . "getting your act together." The Greek New Testament employs a fine word that could easily be rendered "get your act together." The word is *hupotasso,* which is an ethical term literally meaning "to arrange under," "to set in array under." But as soon as one reads the common English translation of *hupotasso* there is the instant threat of lost communication. You see, many of us would literally choke on the word *hupotasso,* "getting your act together," because it is universally translated by the English word "submission."

Did you know that there is a definite doctrine of submission in the New Testament? The word "to submit" appears there at least thirty-five times. It seems painfully obvious, however, that people are reluctant to talk about it. Search the many Bible encyclopedias and dictionaries available today. You will find very little, if any, material on submission. Consult the vast number of exhaustive critical commentaries on the passages teaching submission. Although the word cannot be ignored entirely, its doctrinal significance is rarely, if ever, developed. Let's face it— human beings, who are at heart a rebellious and independent lot, do not like to talk about submission. And any communication on the subject will be costly indeed. Let's pay that price. For a minute, let's consider the doctrine of submission in the Word of God.

THE FACTS OF THE MATTER

The Bible says much more about submission than we might expect. Submission, it should also be insisted, is not a doctrine "for women only," nor is it strictly a domestic issue. God calls every Christian to be submissive in certain crucial areas of his or her life. In a very real sense, being submissive means getting your act together. The apostle Paul reminds each of us that we are to "be subject to one another out of reverence for Christ" (Eph. 5:21). The *Jerusalem Bible* graphically renders this verse, "give way to one another in obedience to Christ." Before engaging in a more detailed examination of how we are to be submissive, let's consider three very basic biblical facts concerning submission.

1. Submission is a private matter of the soul.
2. Submission is a human duty for the good of all men.
3. Submission to authority demands responsibility and discernment—it is never a resignation of moral sense or personal accountability to God.

Nobody's business but yours. In the Greek New Testament, the verb "to submit" never appears in the active voice when descriptive of a Christian duty. We are never commanded to "subdue one another out of reverence for Christ." It never says, "husbands, subdue your wives" or "parents, conquer your kids for Christ." When descriptive of a Christian duty, the verb "to submit" usually appears in a different voice. The middle voice is neither active ("I subdue"), nor is it passive ("I am subdued"). It is expressive of personal advantage; it places special emphasis on the subject of the verb ("I submit myself"). Ephesians 5:21 could be paraphrased, "Place yourself under submission for your own good." To carry the idea further, "Wives, submit yourselves to your husbands and fulfill yourselves."

From this fact it is safe to conclude that submission is God's personal challenge to each of us. It will do little good for a husband to bellow at his wife, "Submit or pay the consequence." Chances are if she refuses to listen to God, she won't be listening to you. It will do little good for parents to scream at their kids, "Submit to me, you little brats." If they refuse to listen to God, chances are they won't listen to you either. (You are much better off to quietly pick up a paddle and help God get the children's attention.)

In the final analysis, only God in his sovereign rule of the human heart through Christ can effectively command us to submit to others. And only the believer in the integrity of his own heart can become submissive through the power of the Holy Spirit. Submission is a private matter of the soul as the believer becomes more and more eager to do as his Lord directs. Because of the private nature of this command and the independent life style of many people today, it is very easy to ignore or dismiss the doctrine of submission. But if you refuse to submit in areas that God calls into question, you may risk the ruin of your life and the lives of those you love most dearly.

I recall with some regret a few years back when a middle-aged woman sat in my office and shared a very sad story. Her husband was an accomplished professional. However, his work took a great toll upon his marriage and his relationship to the children. The home and every concern in that home became expendable to the demands of his work. It was a tragedy, however common. The woman's response was to take charge. She stepped into the vacuum the husband left and became a rather outspoken leader; first, in all matters domestic, and finally in the local church, where she was a major influence. In time she became accustomed to refuting the authority of the elders of her church, and loudly proclaimed her lack of trust in them.

Sadly enough, this became her life style. She loved the Lord and was zealous in her service. And she loved her husband, though she mourned his failure to be what God required. She lost sight of the fact that a submissive spirit is the greatest model of Christian behavior a wife and mother can project for her children. As her children grew older she began to notice an indifference in them to the Lordship of Christ and finally to the gospel itself. Of course, the husband's failure was a large part of the problem. Yet it was tragic to see the wife's growing realization that she had also become part of the problem as she disregarded Scripture's instruction on submission. After twenty years of neglect, what can be said? What magic words can undo the damage? We wept together.

I love humanity, it's just people I can't stand. The second fact regarding submission is that it is a human duty for the good of all men. Although the word "submission" appears over thirty-five times in the New Testament, only twice are we told to submit directly to God: " Submit yourselves therefore to God" (James 4:7); and, "Be subject to the Father of spirits and live" (Heb. 12:9). (It is true that Romans 8:7 speaks of submission to God's law, and 10:3 speaks of submitting to God's righteousness, but these commands work out primarily in human relationships within the community.) Certainly we are to submit to God. He is Lord and King and we are right to call him so. But what does this emphasis on the human aspect of submission mean? It means that we must evaluate our submissiveness by our spirit, not by false piety or devotion. A Christian must evaluate his submission in the light of how he treats others.

Some believers find it easy to "submit to God" as long as they are the final authority in the matter of God's will. But they find it hard to submit to their brothers and sisters—to give way to their opinions. I have a friend whom I admire greatly. He spends hours in prayer each week; he is an aggressive evangelist and a virtual "iron man" of personal devotional discipline. The trouble is, he just doesn't get along with other people. How can this be? For one thing, it is his weakness. We all have them. Some of us are more prone to controversy than others; some of us have to work harder at getting along with others. On the other hand, my friend had grown insensitive to much of what the Bible says regarding Christian growth. He had forgotten that he was to be submissive to his family in Christ. He had mastered many personal skills, but he had overlooked the interpersonal. I wish I were more like him in zeal, service, and discipline. But it is good to remind ourselves that one form of service is submission to God and man. It is a human duty that is played out in concrete terms of giving in to each other.

Stopping the Christian cop-out. The third and perhaps most weighty fact regarding submission in Scripture is that submission to authority demands responsibility and discernment. It is never a resignation of moral sense or personal accountability to God. This is a crucial principle for any thinking person to understand if that person is to reconcile submission with other Christian duties in Scripture. Mankind is essentially a rebellious lot. Men don't like submission to authority unless they can construe it to mean a resignation of their own moral responsibility. So Adam pointed to Eve, and Eve pointed to the snake, and the snake stonewalled it. But God held them all responsible.

Peter, who told us clearly in his letter to "be submissive to your masters with all respect" (1 Peter 2:18), was able, nonetheless, to tell the civil authorities who forbade him to preach Christ: "Whether it is right in the sight of God to listen to you rather than to God, you must judge" (Acts 4:19). Rather than submit, Peter defied the authority that tried to force him into acting against God's desires.

Frankly, the wife who allows child abuse, under the guise of submission to her husband, is guilty before God. The employee who lies for his boss is guilty before God. The citizen who does not protest injustice in his land is guilty before God.

C. S. Lewis was so right when he noted that Satan sends errors into the world in pairs—opposite pairs. His plan, says Lewis, is for his victim to see one evil and run from it blindly into the arms of its opposite extreme. Many conservative Christians find it too easy to practice a mindless submission to authority. The other side of the coin is the more liberal Christian who finds it so easy to protest and resist any authority over him. It seems we either have churches blindly following their leaders, no matter what, or we have churches who don't follow anyone.

God's path appears to be the middle path: the balanced walk. It is a walk that is careful, attentive, informed, and committed. Before commanding submission in Ephesians 5:21, Paul clearly said, "Look carefully then how you walk, not as unwise men but as wise" (5:15). When we submit we never lay aside our discernment and our responsibility.

THREE GREAT ARENAS

God has given men three great human institutions: the state, the church, and the family. The New Testament teaches that submission is to be expressed within those three institutions. When we consider submission in these three areas we are at the heart of the doctrine of submission in Scripture.

Submission at first glance. Let's first consider submission and the state. Romans 13:1-7 is a crucial passage in the understanding of this question.

Let every person be subject to the governing authorities. For there is no authority except from God, and those that exist have been instituted by God. Therefore he who resists the authorities resists what God has appointed, and those who resist will incur judgment. For rulers are not a terror to good conduct, but to bad. Would you have no fear of him who is in authority? Then do what is good, and you will receive his approval, for he is God's servant for your good. But if you do wrong, be afraid, for he does not bear the sword in vain; he is the servant of God to execute his wrath on the wrongdoer. Therefore one must be subject, not only to avoid God's wrath but also for the sake of conscience. For the same reason you also pay taxes, for the authorities are ministers of God, attending to this very thing. Pay all of them their dues, taxes to whom taxes are due, revenue to whom revenue is due, respect to whom respect is due, honor to whom honor is due.

From government to God. Two things seem apparent here. The first is that human government is instituted by God. The second is that in its proper functioning, human government expresses God's sovereign management of the world. Acts 17:26, 27 further accentuates this:

And he [God] made from one every nation of men to live on all the face of the earth, having determined allotted periods and the boundaries of their habitation, that they should seek God, in the hope that they might feel after him and find him. Yet he is not far from each one of us . . . .

The unavoidable connection between man's response to God by faith and the proper function of government is not often noted. Good government conditions us to respond to a good God. Men are tempted to doubt the justice and mercy of God if the state does not prefigure these qualities. Thus, as men wisely submit to human government, they are developing responses which will enable them to submit to God. As we observe others being submissive to the governing authorities, we are instructed regarding obedience to God.

In many systems of prophecy it is taught that in the last days demonic forces will be unleashed which will cause the collapse of government (Rev. 16:13, 14). Satan hates good government. This, it seems obvious, is the reason why Scripture so often calls the Christian to respect and submit to governing authorities.

God set up national sovereignties, and when men ignore these boundaries, and in quest of power and glory, "nations rise up against nations," they are really rising up against God. Whether we refer to the cold and ruthless rule of Rome, the insane power lust of Napoleon, or the wicked conquests of Hitler, God is the one who is opposed by the cases of indifference to national sovereignty. It is not surprising that Rome epitomized the inhuman cruelty of ancient paganism. Nor is it surprising that Napoleon rose from the godless evils of the French Revolution, or that Hitler desired to rid the West not only of God's people, Israel, but also of the "superstitions" of Christianity. These empires or would-be empires were fighting God as well as man. They violated God's moral boundaries as well as the boundaries of other nations.

In the light of Scripture it is hard to deny that Christians have drawn too harsh a division between the state and the church. Human government is not necessarily worldly, and the truly dangerous tension is between the church and the world, not church and state. Christians should see to it that human government does not become too worldly. To many of us who were weaned on the maxim of separation of church and state, this sounds vaguely like heresy. But the separation between church and state was never intended to be a separation between God and state. Christians should draw the battle line between the "world" and themselves, not between political institutions and themselves.

WATERGATE AND YOU. A basic problem in submission to government is the question of corruption in high office. What happens when human government becomes corrupt? The sad answer is that righteous men suffer, and they had better seek the face of God in prayer. If human government becomes corrupt, the righteous must never participate in that evil, whether it is racism, oppression, an unjust war, or any other immorality. God still requires his people to behave morally and responsibly. And they will undoubtedly suffer opposition in a world in which immoral demands are imposed by a corrupted authority.

Nonetheless, it is clear that Christians are commanded to submit to human government. Consider 1 Timothy 2:1-4:

First of all, then, I urge that supplications, prayers, intercessions, and thanksgivings, be made for all men, for kings and all who are in high positions, that we may lead a quiet and peaceable life, and respectful in every way. This is good, and it is acceptable in the sight of God our Savior, who desires all men to be saved and to come to the knowledge of the truth.

To refrain from speaking evil of our leaders, and to seek God's favor and guidance for them, is part of the responsible submission to human government which God requires of all believers in Christ. If one needs a reason beyond the simple command of God, perhaps it is hinted at in Exodus 22:28: "You shall not revile God, nor curse a ruler of your people." Have you ever wondered about the connection between our attitude toward God and our attitude toward human government? They are inextricably woven together. A man who is unsubmissive to government is conditioning himself to be unsubmissive to God, and he is also conditioning all those who are dearest to him.

Could it be possible that in mindless slander of leadership (a favorite American pastime) we are becoming more and more prone to slander God? The ultimate tragedy of Watergate was a theological one. Many Americans have been made more prone to slander God since our leaders behaved so badly. The truth is, God requires our submission to human government in order for us to fulfill the great commandment, in order to love God more and more, with soul, mind, heart, and strength.

Sharpening submission's focus: the church. We read in Ephesians 5:21 that we are to be in mutual submission to one another as a general ground rule for Christian fellowship. We must cultivate a submissive spirit whether we are in leadership or under leadership, whether we are the head of the home or in submission in the home.

Submission in the local church is explained in Scripture as having basic functions. The first is one of submission to leadership.

Obey your leaders and submit to them; for they are keeping watch over your souls, as men who will have to give account. Let them do this joyfully, and not sadly, for that would be of no advantage to you (Heb. 13:17).

But we beseech you, brethren, to respect those who labor among you and are over you in the Lord and admonish you, and to esteem them very highly in love because of their work (1 Thess. 5:12, 13).

Let the elders who rule well be considered worthy of double honor, especially those who labor in preaching and teaching; for the scripture says, "You shall not muzzle an ox when it is treading out the grain," and, "The laborer deserves his wages." Never admit any charge agaist an elder except on the evidence of two or three witnesses (1 Tim. 5:17-19).

The thought of having someone "over" us seems to run against the grain of a basic Protestant mindset. Nevertheless, who is over you in the Lord? There are to be leaders in the church who are over us. Notice, by the way, that the word is plural. This is not an appeal to set up a single "church boss," nor is it an invitation to be selective as to which of the church leaders you will deign to obey. Every believer is to be in submission to the God-appointed leadership of the local church. This includes the individual leaders themselves.

The second function of the church in which submission is required is corporate worship. We must be submissive in our worship. There is to be a melding of spiritual gifts and orderly conduct. Our submission is also expressed in sensitive respect for the needs and gifts of others. Our submissive spirit is displayed not only in the exercise of spiritual gifts and in a willingness to control ourselves for the good of the whole church; it is expressed as well in a teachable spirit. We must be willing to learn as we are instructed in sound doctrine by elders who rule and teach as pastors in the church.

A DIFFICULT PASSAGE (1 Cor. 14). Submission in public worship

is the basic assumption of Paul's teaching in 1 Corinthians 14:26-40.
Let's consider this passage.

What then, brethren? When you come together, each one has a
hymn, a lesson, a revelation, a tongue, or an interpretation. Let
all things be done for edification. If any speak in a tongue let
there be only two or at most three, and each in turn; and let one
interpret. But if there is no one to interpret, let each of them
keep silence in church and speak to himself and to God. Let two
or three prophets speak, and let the others weigh what is said. If
a revelation is made to another sitting by, let the first be silent.
For you can all prophesy one by one, so that all may learn and
all be encouraged; and the spirits of prophets are subject to
prophets. For God is not a God of confusion but of peace. As in
all the churches of the saints, the women should keep silence in
the churches. For they are not permitted to speak, but should be
subordinate, as even the law says. If there is anything they desire
to know, let them ask their husbands at home. For it is shameful
for a woman to speak in church. What! Did the word of God
originate with you, or are you the only ones it has reached? If
any one thinks that he is a prophet, or spiritual, he should
acknowledge that what I am writing to you is a command of the
Lord. If any one does not recognize this, he is not recognized.
So, my brethren, earnestly desire to prophesy, and do not forbid
speaking in tongues; but all things should be done decently and
in order.

There is a great deal of information here that is difficult to
understand. We should observe that the aspect of the worship
service in focus here is the instructional activity of the church.
Five things are specifically mentioned in verse 26: a psalm (a
theological poem used for instruction, much like the inspired
hymn of Philippians 2:5-11)[1], a teaching, a revelation, a tongue,
and an interpretation. Since a tongue is not to be shared in the
church without clear interpretation, we can safely reduce this to
four sources of instruction.

DUAL CONTROLS. It is clear from this passage that in the
church, even with regard to the most spiritual times of worship,
there is still to be external control. When Paul orders, "let all
things be done for edification," or "let one interpret," or "let him

keep silent," obviously these commands are addressed to those who are in leadership and control the worship service. It is equally obvious that the worshipers are to be submissive to their authority.

Not only is an external control commanded of our worship, but also an internal control (14:32). The prophets are to have control over their gifts and their messages. Mindless babblings were the mark of pagan worship in Corinth and the vestiges of Canaanite worship in Palestine. There must be personal discipline of the human spirit in worship. There is to be mind-controlled as well as spirit-controlled worship. We are never mindlessly to relinquish control of our mouth in public worship. Whatever tongues *are*, then, at least in 1 Corinthians 14, they are never a mindless, thought-suspended activity. In worship there is to be an external control calling for submission and an internal control calling for submission. This is a submission to the realities of personal discipline.

A LESSON IN SILENCE. In 1 Corinthians 14 it says specifically that women are to be "silent" regarding the instructional gifts which are to be exercised in the local church. This seems to be a clear application of 1 Timothy 2:12: "I permit no woman to teach or to have authority over men; she is to keep silent." We should note, however, that the word "quiet" of 1 Timothy (*hesachia*) differs greatly from the word "silent" (*sigao*) of 1 Corinthians. The word "quiet" refers to all Christians, male or female, in 1 Timothy 2:2, and describes a gentleness which should be a mark of the Lord Jesus in every believer's life.

The word "silent" means to be mute, and has significance only when it puts a stop to unauthorized speaking, whether it is the confusion of tongues with no interpreter, or a competition of prophets shouting over one another to be heard, or a woman seeking to instruct men in the church. It is in the area of women assuming spiritual authority in the church that there is the clear apostolic command of submission to male authority. Why is this? The answer is not in the so-called rabbinic anti-feminism of Paul, but in the theological significance of the sex roles lived out in the two great schools for theological truth, the church and the home.

There can be no question that Scripture acknowledges the essential equality of the sexes: "There is neither Jew nor Greek, there is neither slave nor free, there is neither male nor female; for you are all one in Christ Jesus" (Gal. 3:28). Still, it can only be denied with the greatest of interpretative gymnastics (unless you attack the integrity of Scripture itself) that the Bible teaches a "functional" submission of woman to man in church and home.

The Bible does indeed teach such a submission. In 1 Corinthians 11:3, while describing the order of private worship in the home (Paul does not begin instructing in public worship until verse 17) the apostle clearly teaches: "But I want you to understand that the head of every man is Christ, and the head of a woman is her husband, and the head of Christ is God." Notice the complete entwining of spiritual and physical roles in that verse. Notice as well that there are three relationships spelled out, but only one of them is visible. Paul talks of Christ's relationship with man (invisible); Christ's relationship to God (invisible); and man's relationship to woman (visible).

We will develop this in more detail later, but it seems clear that a woman has a unique sexual role in that she, like the tip of an iceberg, suggests in her physical submission to authority a great hidden truth concerning the preeminent majesty of God and the irresistible necessity for mankind to submit to that majesty. A man submits to Christ, as Christ submits himself to God the Father. And woman, in her submission in church and home, becomes a living picture of love. We must insist that the woman serves a great theological truth, not a cultural hangup, when she is submissive to her husband and refrains from ruling men in the church. The woman becomes a teacher by not teaching, a leader by not leading; and her best pupils are those she is to love most, her brothers and sisters in Christ (the church) and her own children and husband (the family).

The woman in submission is in good company since Christ, though he is God, and equal with God the Father, willingly submitted himself in functional terms within the Godhead. Theologians have long acknowledged in the Trinity the difference between functional subordination and essential equality. Human sexuality is one of the strongest expressions of the Godhead. We have been made, male and female, in the image of God (Gen. 1:27). A reversal of sex roles, such as occurs in homosexuality, will forfeit what can be known about God (Rom. 1:25, 26). It is definitely stated in Romans 1 that a tampering with the clear, natural revelation of God resulted in a confusion of the sex roles. There is an undeniable connection between knowledge of the Trinity and proper sexual expression. The two evidently share the same mysterious qualities of equal union and willing submission. The nature of such relationships is a mystery, according to Paul (Eph. 5:22-28). We have here, nonetheless, a true comparison.

WHEN THE WOMAN TEACHES BEST. Both Ephesians 5 and 1 Corinthians 11 ascribe to the woman the role of a model believer. This is what Paul means in 1 Corinthians 11:7 when he says, "[the male] is the image and glory of God; but the woman is the glory of man." Paul does not mean that the woman exists merely to enhance a man like some sort of decoration. No! She is to embody the highest picture of humanity in her sexual role. Glory is a word often used to describe the physical presence of God. Man in his sexual role is a picture of God the Father, and a woman, being the highest expression of humanity, becomes, in her submission, a picture of how one submits to a loving, gracious God.

The woman in submission in church and home teaches us all how to be obedient children of God. This is particularly true of her children. Take a person who is unsubmissive and rebellious toward God, or the church, or the state, and many times you will find that person had a mother who refused to be a submissive wife. Perhaps she thus led her child away from Christ, and didn't even realize that this was going on. With all the threats of this world against healthy human sexuality and proper respect of authority, we must learn and obey the order of God or risk the loss of our own children. We must not abandon them to the whirlpool of rebellion and heartbroken confusion that is characteristic of our modern society.

Submission's sharpest focus: the home. The third, and perhaps greatest of all God-given institutions in which submission is to be a key dynamic, is the family. The family structure assumed in the New Testament is somewhat foreign to us since it has as its model the Hellenistic pattern of the Greek-speaking world.

SLAVES AND SUBMISSION. In such a household, slaves were considered a legitimate part of the family unit. Consequently, in several places in the New Testament, slaves are encouraged to be submissive to their masters. In the Western world, thank God,

legal slavery is gone. In the modern world, as in the ancient
world, the single strongest force in its overthrow was Christianity.
But while slavery held men in its complex grasp, the New
Testament sought to bring healing and help to those so
oppressed. The slave was taught submission and the master was
taught compassion. The model for both was the "Master-slave,"
Jesus Christ. Though the truth of Christianity finally succeeded in
crushing slavery, there remain applications of the submission of
slave to master which relate to our modern era. The admonition
to the slave reminds all of us that God requires from us diligence,
dependability, faithfulness, and hard work. These qualities should
mark a believer who owes his employer respect. Likewise, the
employer is clearly taught that God requires from him a personal
concern for the well-being of his employee which should extend
beyond mere contractual obligations, in the same way that God's
concern and compassion extend to us (Eph. 6:5-9; 1 Cor. 7:21-24;
Col. 3:22-25; 1 Tim. 6:11-21, Titus 2:9-10; Philemon).

REBELLION MAY BE HAZARDOUS TO YOUR HEALTH. In the family,
children are to be submissive to their parents. The New
Testament gives them a role model: "[Jesus] went down with [his
parents] and came to Nazareth, and was obedient to them"
(Luke 2:51). In Ephesians, Paul reminds us, "Children, obey
your parents in the Lord, for this is right. 'Honor your father and
mother' (this is the first commandment with a promise)" (6:1, 2).
The commandment promises long life (Exod. 20:12).

Someone once wisely said "Don't hate your parents, because
you are going to grow up to be just like them." A child who
never learns to honor his parents will develop a profound sense
of self-loathing. A child who is repeatedly provoked to anger by
his parents will forever be his own most relentless adversary. The
relationship between such mental conflict and physical health
may possibly be the basis for the promise of Ephesians 6:1, 2.

HERE COMES THE BRIDE. The Bible teaches that in the home, as
in the church, women are to be submissive to their own husbands
(Eph. 5; 1 Cor. 11; see above). The church and the home are the
only two areas in which Scripture commands the unique
submission of women to men. This is not a norm for the
marketplace, or the academy, or any other area of human
activity. We have already noted and will later develop more fully
the fact that the reasons for this are theological, not cultural.

In every area of submission it is first a private matter for the wife to deal with. Scripture addresses the wife, telling her to submit; the husband is never instructed to "subdue her." In her submission the wife follows a great role model:

For to this you have been called, because Christ also suffered for you, leaving you an example, that you should follow in his steps. He committed no sin; no guile was found on his lips. When he was reviled, he did not revile in return; when he suffered, he did not threaten; but he trusted to him who judges justly. He himself bore our sins in his Body on the tree, that we might die to sin and live to righteousness. By his wounds you have been healed. For you were straying like sheep, but have now returned to the Shepherd and Guardian of your souls, Likewise [e.g. just like Jesus] you wives, be submissive to your husbands . . . (1 Peter 2:21—3:1).

A wife's submission in the home is also a human duty to help others. It is not to make things comfortable for the man. Rather the wife's submission helps all believers (though chiefly her own family) to properly understand the depth of commitment God desires of man.

Finally, the submission of the wife in the home must never mean a submission to what is wrong or immoral. How well I remember the sad story of a Christian wife whose non-Christian husband encouraged her to extend her sexual favors to a business associate in order to help the husband close a big deal. No adherence to submission should ever require a wife to break an even higher law of God.

The idea of submission of the wife to her husband has been greatly maligned. In part this is true because of much misinformation on the matter. We should reject as thoroughly nonbiblical those who teach the universal submission of all women to all men at all times and in all places. We should reject as nonbiblical those who foolishly demand submission in areas of personal privilege or matters of taste and style. If a husband demands that his wife wear a particular color and the wife feels she would rather not wear it, that husband would be foolish to force the issue—as well as decidedly unbiblical. A wife's true submission, if controlled by God's Word, can be a great healing and saving force in the family. More will be said on this when we consider the woman's role in Scripture.

THE BOTTOM LINE. Though much attention in this discussion has been given to the issue of feminine submission within the sexual role, the doctrine of submission extends far beyond that important aspect. Submission as defined in Scripture is a powerful, creative force which can mold all our lives in a closer conformity to Christ. That has been the goal of this general statement of the doctrine of submission.

But after the spade work is done on a biblical doctrine, there comes a time to lay the dictionaries down and push the papers back, close our eyes, and think. We don't have to do this long before the idea of submisson breaks out of its linguistic corral. Submission becomes "rights we refuse to exercise for a higher purpose." Submission is love that doesn't seek its own way. Submission is the blessedness of one persecuted for righteousness' sake. Submission is Jesus emptying himself of all but love. Submission is the cheek that is turned against an angry fist, or the silence that greets an angry word. Submission is the mile walked beyond the law's demand. Submission is the cross Christ endured, and it is the cross the Christian is told to take up every day.

In short, submission is the Christian life. It takes on different forms for different people; we all have different responsibilities, different roles, and different callings. But submission is the same for all of us who bear the name of Jesus. "Be submissive to each other, out of reverence for Christ."

POINT-COUNTERPOINT

George: We say in this chapter that there is an undeniable connection between knowledge of the Trinity and proper sexual expression. I want you to correct me if I am getting off base theologically, but isn't it true that we submit to God first, and that such a submission is expressed *almost totally* in our human relationships? When I was thinking of that in terms of marriage, it seemed that marriage implied three, and not merely two interested parties—the husband, the wife, and God. As Christians, we know further that the Holy Spirit indwells our bodies. In fact, 1 Corinthians 6 gives the indwelling Spirit's presence as a rationale for avoiding sexual abuse. Once again, we are counseled to consider the "third Person" involved in every human relationship. So our knowledge of the Trinity would caution us against viewing marriage as simply a sexual union between two autonomous selves. Instead, God revealed to us that we were created male and female in his image. And thus the marriage relationship is intended to be a picture for us of the relationship that Christ has with the church. So the intimate relationship between husband and wife could never be complete without the three persons—man, woman, and God.

Mike: I think you put your finger on a very important aspect of the theology of personal relationships, namely the role God plays as the inevitable third party in every human encounter. We are skirting the edges of disaster when we ignore the theological realities that govern human relationships. Man, both in his inner constitution and in his relationship with others, is a very complex and precise instrument, and he tampers with God's fundamental principles for human behavior at the risk of grave personality distortion.

George: I appreciated what you said about those fundamental principles when you pointed out the necessity to understand the doctrine of submission in its fuller context. It's wrong to consider the marriage relationship the only area of our lives requiring personal submission. Submission is essential to good government, and to effective churches, as well as to happy homes. These different levels of submission, however, are more intertwined than we might think at first glance. For example, the state, which God has ordained and which is an institution to which we have an obligation to be submissive, is also the agency which regulates the legal marriage relationship.

Mike: It becomes crucial to acknowledge the fact that the various arenas for submission do not and must not function independently of one another. When operating properly, they intertwine and catch us up in a whole context of interrelationships. This network demands sensitivity to God's requirements, to personal concerns as well as to the collective needs of men. We must never consider man separated from God just as we must never rip the state, as it were, from God's hands altogether. And it is equally true that we must never remove personal relationships or personal preferences or personal activities totally from state concern, interest, and even regulation. There seem to be a great number of voices today calling for a removal of God and state and a removal of "personal preferences" from state interest and control. I'm worried that what we'll end up with is a very powerful, godless, and impersonal state. This seems to be against the very spirit of Western democracy.

George: Given the intertwining of relationships between the institutions of the state and church and marriage, I can see why you said in this chapter that Satan hates good government. You pointed out that he would prefer a godless and impersonal state. The definition of a good government would be one which would conform to God's will, reinforce the institution of marriage, and allow the full expression of the church in freedom. Part of our obligation for submission within the church involves initiating a new marriage in public. The church service solemnizing marriage thereby teaches us that marriage is not a totally private matter between husband and wife. In fact, the state authorizes the clergyman to sign the couple's marriage license. So to be submissive to the church as well as to the state requires that the couple acknowledge that the marriage is not even a private matter between God and themselves.

I couldn't help noting the contrast between your discussion of the biblical teaching on submission and the humanistic mindset we described earlier. Submission seems to be diametrically opposed to the kind of independence and self-assertiveness espoused by the philosophy of humanists and radical feminists. In fact, it occurred to me that if a person considered himself, rather than God, the center of the universe, he could never develop a rationale for being truly submissive. He would value submission only in a manipulative sense. In other words, he would think strictly in terms of what he might get out of the relationship. In this next chapter, we're going to see that this is exactly what is happening in our society today. On the other hand, the kind of submission necessary for a stable marriage enduring over many years would need a better rationale than the humanists' world view. As soon as momentary, pragmatic reasons evaporated, the whole humanistic argument for giving way to your spouse would dry up. This is an open invitation to frequent and inevitable conflicts between two self-serving, independent units who lack a continuing bond outside themselves.

Mike: The Bible says that the natural man doesn't accept, appreciate, or ever fully understand the things of the Spirit of God. I think that what you're pointing out is true of the secular humanists, including the radical feminists. To such people, any thought of personal submission would be heinous, a hateful thing. Yet to the biblically sensitive mind, submission is a pathway to blessing, harmony, and great personal fulfillment, if I dare use that much abused word. I should point out that Christians are often to blame for giving ammunition to secular adversaries through improper understanding and practice of submission. Though I know we want to look more closely now at the marriage relationship, we must think of submission in its broadest context of Scripture first, lest we open ourselves up to the misunderstanding that submission is merely a method for male dominance in the marriage relationship. In reality, submission as a Christian duty is much broader and all-inclusive than that. It is a much broader scope than the marriage relationship or the feminine role. But having said that, let's look more closely now at the marriage relationship, a relationship which appears to be under siege.

SIX
MARRIAGE UNDER SIEGE:
Contemporary Challenges
to a Faithful Marriage

In the last chapter we took a long look at the doctrine of
submission according to the New Testament. Admittedly, the
implications of that doctrine run far beyond the concerns of
human sexuality and the proper function of the family. But
having laid the groundwork, let us now consider the fierce
challenges that face most marriages today. As we do so, we must
realize that it is the doctrine of submission that will provide the
strength to resist the destructive forces that Satan is throwing
against marriage today. As the husband and wife learn to submit
to the Lordship of Christ and thus live in humble, loving
submission to each other, the marriage will endure, the family
will stand, and God's purposes for women and men will be
preserved.

As God's intentions for marriage are fulfilled in the mutual
submission of family members, forces of considerable spiritual
power are released into the marital union.

Within a Christian framework of submission, a healthy respect
for authority is born. Both parent and child are reinforced in
learning to give honor to human authorities and in behaving
honorably when they assume positions of authority. Most
importantly, the home becomes the key instrument instructing us
all to accept and love the authority God rightly exerts over our
lives.

The doctrine of submission, when learned within the context of a Christian marriage, provides a basis of relationship that is infinitely more consistent to loving commitment then the self-centered demands of many humanistic "experiments" such as contract marriages and living agreements. As we exercise submission we learn the great values of self-sacrificial commitments which enhance every aspect of balanced family life.

Although 40 percent of all marriages now end in divorce, the Christian can boldly anticipate a different destiny for his or her marriage. The destructive tragedy of divorce can be reversed by sensitive obedience to God's teaching on submission.

The age-old dilemma of parents demanding, futilely, that children "do as they say, not as they do," can be done away with when those parents discover God's path of submission and become true examples of good behavior. The doctrine of submission offers the family effective models for constructive child rearing and provides for consistency between parents' words and actions.

In this chapter we will see how so many marriage relationships suffer from a lack of all these things. We will further see how God's program for marriage successfully counters the wicked plans of the evil one.

MODERN ARGUMENTS AGAINST MARRIAGE

The revolt against the traditional view of submission in married life is most obvious in the wholesale practice of marital infidelity. One would assume that thinking people should agree that the violations of the marriage vows run counter to the natural order of the universe. The epidemic of VD alone should shock modern Americans into enough sensibility to reevaluate the importance of lifelong marriage as an exclusive relationship for sexual expression. The propaganda of pornography loudly blasts its deceiving message that sexual fulfillment can flourish in the ashes of marital fidelity. The humanistic thinkers ignore the mammoth problems of extramarital affairs, VD, and pornography to such an extent that they border on criminal naiveté.[1] Their superficial dogmas are in actuality insidious arguments against marriage. Their views become a cancer that gnaws away whatever hopes our society has for human happiness and harmony.

A badge of honor. One line of argument against the social ideal
of permanent marriage relationships is the theory that second
marriages are more fulfilling than first marriages. According to
this line of thinking, the couple learns a lot "the first time around,"
and by the time they are divorced and embarking on second
marriages they are much more experienced and wise than people
getting married for the first time. Supposedly, someone who has
been divorced has learned that there is no Hollywood ideal on
earth and is better able to adjust to reality because of his or her
divorce. The divorce certificate is like a badge of honor that one
wears which he perhaps might even be tempted to display on the
wall like a college degree. With this line of thinking also comes
the idea that premarital sex better prepares a person for marital
sex.

As appalling as this line of thinking may be, some modern
researchers have attempted to support it. A Princeton University
psychologist even went so far as to conduct a study among
twenty families in which the spouses were previously divorced.[2]
This Princeton study, involving very few people, concluded that
divorce, far from being a social problem itself, is a solution to the
various problems that marriage can produce. In one bold stroke,
the disease is made the cure.

This line of reasoning against marriage can be simply refuted.
Dr. Amitai Etzioni[3] pointed out that numerous research studies
have demonstrated that people dismantle their second marriages
much more often than they do first marriages. In the 1960s, a
third of first marriages ended in divorce, whereas half of second
marriages ended in divorce. More recent statistics of the 1970s
show that 40 percent of first marriages end in divorce and 44
percent of second marriages end in divorce. Though the divorce
rate is higher today than in the past decade, the trend is still the
same. Being divorced is certainly no credential for future marital
stability.

The dotted line. A second line of argument against the
traditional value of marriage is the concept of "trial marriage"
or temporary marriage contracts. Here a new idea is advanced
that we should replace the traditional marriage with a contract
much like other business contracts which can run out.

Those who prefer temporary contracts, as opposed to lifelong marriages, speciously point out that the early colonists in America lived to an average age of twenty-eight or twenty-nine years. This meant that, at most, a marriage would last only ten years before one of the marriage partners would die. In today's world, they say, we have much longer life spans, and lifelong marriages mean as many as fifty years of marriage instead of ten years (as though fifty-year marriages were unheard of before the twentieth century). The obvious foolishness of this argument is painfully apparent. They go on to insist that some kind of "escape clause" should be built in, providing optional, renewable terms for a marriage. The idea is that one would get married for a five- or a ten-year trial period, agreeing in advance on what would happen to the children, what would happen to the stereo set, or what would happen to the family dog in the event that the marriage were not renewed after the initial period. The contract could specify many other things such as agreements on who should take out the garbage, who should wash the dishes, and the like. Those believing in these temporary marriage contracts suppose that they are simply extending the idea of contracts from other areas of human life to the marriage relationship. In reality, they are reducing marriage to nothing more than a contract. Marriage, intended to be a loving, personal, and lifelong relationship, sealed in society by a contract, is thus reduced to an arbitrary legal union.

The critics of the temporary marriage contract point out that a couple in love might not survive the mere exercise of contract negotiations. Is it possible for people in love who want to be together to contemplate who should take possession of their material belongings and eventual children five years hence, when all they are thinking about at the moment is living together in love and harmony?

Critics also point out that marriage built on love, submission, and self-sacrifice should be antagonistic to such negotiations of self-interest.[4] For example, in a contract you could specify such things as the number of hospital visits the husband would make if the wife ended up with a chronic illness. But a married person in love would want to set no quotas on how many visits he would make to a hospital or how many months he would be willing to support a partner who is seriously ill. True love is a commitment and a desire that the marriage bond be permanent, "until death do us part," which exists "for better or worse." What kind of love would it be if it were specified in the contract that the marriage bond exists "until three months of continuous hospitalization do us part," or that the marriage contract will exist "for better, but not for worse, if worse consists of more than four weeks in duration"?

Marriage is a personal commitment bond, and attempts to reduce it to a contract actually make it something less than marriage. The logic of contracting reciprocal obligations may work in business, but it will not work for the marriage relationship.[5] The very essence of the marriage relationship is that each member gives up part of his own sovereignty to the other in self-sacrificing mutual submission. The marriage relationship is *not* a mere contract between two sovereign individuals who have given up no territory to the other.

A contract assumes two sovereign and independent individuals who are entering into a legally binding agreement with various conditions on one another's performance in the future. But the marriage relationship has always been assumed to be one in which the two members become one unit and thereby give up some degree of individual sovereignty in favor of a mutual submission to one another for shared existence over a lifetime.

One of the most blatant violations of the concept of marriage is the recent trend for courts to declare that if a woman is pregnant and wants an abortion, she need not inform her husband of the pregnancy and of her decision for the abortion. Such a law or its interpretation is treating the woman as though she is ultimately a single unit who has not given up any part of her individual sovereignty. A true marriage relationship would require the consultation, advice, and consent of the husband regarding the couples' child.

Is marriage outmoded? A third line of reasoning against the traditional marriage unit asserts that the extended family justified the existence of marriage. It did so by providing a social connection of concerned relatives who united to provide mutual assistance. In the past, aunts, uncles, and grandparents cared for the various personal needs of individuals in "the family."

Today the large majority of American families are no longer part of extended families. This is due in part to our ever-growing, mobile, transient, and impersonalized technocratic society. We do not have the kind of extended families we once did. Consequently, marriage appears to some to be an outmoded anachronism.

In response to this it can be noted that, in the first place, marriage created the extended family, not vice versa. If there is any force that could possibly reverse the admitted evil of our impersonalized society it would be healthy marriages, building up our fragmented network of personal concern. If the good of an extended family has been damaged by impersonal pressure, it hardly follows that we should abandon the last bastion of personal caring units—marriage. That is, of course, unless we would accept this cruel isolationism as a social good and a welcomed fruit of progress.

It's more fun to be one. A fourth argument against the concept of a permanent marriage and family unit is the logical extension of the humanistic emphasis on individual hedonism. It is very common for Americans in the last half of the twentieth century to believe that the full happiness of the individual is the most important thing in the world. The "rugged idealism" of the American frontiersman has been translated into the selfish philosophy that is rampant in today's society.[6] This philosophy places the individual's happiness above all other values, such as commitment to the family and submission in marriage.

The unbounded quest for *individual* fulfillment is working against the traditional concept of marriage. Marriage relationships and family relationships have always been based, in part, on the self-sacrificing bond of submission of each individual member to one another. It was never the idea of traditional marriage for the partners to calculate a balance sheet at the end of each month to determine whether or not the benefit from the relationship was worth the investment of time, money, energy, and emotion.

Somehow the American concept of business transaction has once again been applied to the marriage relationship. Some feel if they are investing $2000 worth of resources into the marriage they should expect at least $2000 worth of benefits back from the marriage. And if they don't get it back, they would be justified in terminating the relationship. As with any business venture, if the investment turns sour and there runs a period of meager returns for the investment, then the idea is that the person is justified in pulling out of a bad deal. A businessman might sell an old machine that is no longer functioning optimally, in favor of buying a new one. In the same way, many people now accept the idea of trading in an old spouse, who is no longer as exciting as he or she used to be, in favor of a new one. The idea is that if we must submit and sacrifice too much, then the marriage relationship isn't really worth it, so we may as well chuck that one and find a new one before "time runs out."

A mother with an infant may decide that being up every night on the hour is just not worth it. She may decide that she is not getting enough gratification or fulfillment out of the relationship with the infant, compared to the tremendous investment she has in the relationship. Whatever happened to the idea of self-sacrifice for another family member? Many mothers now value a career over the natural biological function of nurturing an infant. Often the decision to "drop out" is made on purely hedonistic values. The woman simply asks, "Am *I* being totally fulfilled in this relationship? Could *I* be fulfilled more if I escaped the demands of motherhood for most of the day?"

This new approach to marriage extends the same kind of selfish attitude to the man and wife relationship. Instead of being sensitive, caring, submissive, and giving toward the marriage partner, each asks, "How much am I getting out of this relationship?" If one is not getting as much out of the relationship as he is putting into it, then this outlook would lead him to walk away from the commitment.

The seeking of self-fulfillment in a blind hedonistic way is doomed to failure. This whole approach totally ignores a fact which is woven into the structure of the universe. It may be simply stated as: "Satisfaction comes in serving something bigger than ourselves."[7]

If the marriage relationship exists by contract or if it is built on a succession of divorce certificates as credentials, or if it is simply abandoned because it is no longer logistically possible to maintain an extended family unit, what does that say about us? That we have lost, as a human race, the capacity to obtain satisfaction from giving to others, from submitting to one another, from caring about others. We have lost the joy of living for something much bigger than the moment. We have lost the ability to delay gratification for a greater good. Instead, we have sold out to a temporary strategy of getting all we can at the moment and ignoring the future. This means ignoring our future and our children's, if we are so casual about terminating relationships between a child's biological mother and father.

The paradox is clear: The individual who pursues the basic drive to maximize his or her own self-gratification as quickly as possible is doomed to failure. Human fulfillment cannot be directly sought as an end in itself. Fulfillment is a by-product of self-sacrifice and giving, caring for and loving others in mutually submissive relationships.

If the traditional marriage relationship is abandoned by our American society in favor of a self-serving value system, we have lost not only the possibility of our own fulfillment, but the potential for fulfillment in the next generation as well. We may have succeeded in destroying the very foundation of civilized life.

The Dr. Jekyll syndrome. America seems to be suffering from a severe case of "cognitive dissonance." On the one hand, the average citizen in our country would decry the obvious evils of the rising divorce rate, short-term marriages, and the more blatant philosophies of the self-serving humanist. But, on the other hand, he shows considerable tolerance toward, and even an occasional participatory interest in, the accelerated immorality all around him. The average American is torn by this immoral ambivalence to the point that his creeds and his conduct are in dangerous conflict.

Most Americans might say that marriage is a good idea, just as they automatically agree that motherhood, apple pie, and the American flag are good things. But to find out what a person really thinks about marriage, we need to look at his actions. What kinds of actions reveal people's true values concerning marriage? It might be somewhat unpopular to display a bumper sticker saying, "Abolish marriage," but certain actions in effect say just that. Actions such as: sexual relations outside of marriage; "wife swapping"; involvement in pornography. Very few Americans actually say, "marriages should be done away with." Those who do are quite often attempting to rationalize their own marital failures. The vast majority of Americans who speak against the value of marriage are speaking by their actions, rather than by their words.

TWO ENEMIES OF MARRIAGE: PROMISCUITY AND PORNOGRAPHY

The traditonal view of marriage included the exclusive contract for sexual intimacy between the couple. Virginity before marriage was expected. Sexual fidelity after marriage was the norm. But people have been voting against marriage, not so much by word, but by deed. An escalating revolt against the traditional view of marriage is obvious in the growth of the pornography industry and in the various indicators of growing promiscuity, including: the skyrocketing divorce rate in the second half of the twentieth century; the increasing rate of illegitimate births; and the new trend toward "living together" as a substitute for marriage.

Promiscuous pressures. It has become fashionable in American society to belittle the virgin as a "sexually inexperienced" individual. A lifetime commitment of sexual fidelity to one's married partner is no longer the universal expectation. Marriages are now often viewed as temporary contracts which are kept as long as they "work out." If either partner experiences stress or a change of "taste," many modern Americans now expect that partner to dissolve the marriage relationship and pursue other relationships, so as not to "waste" the few short years of youthful attractiveness to the opposite sex

In the popular way of thinking, the idea that a woman should be sexually faithful to her husband is no longer part of the ideal feminine role. Similarly, some people glorify sexual escapades as a "masculine" endeavor in which the man "conquers" woman after woman to prove his virility. Each sexual conquest is somehow viewed as another notch on the masculine belt, so to speak. Many people view the idea of sexual fidelity to a marriage partner as quaint, if not downright naive.[8]

VD: A HARSH REALITY. What is the result of our open revolt against marriage? Should our democracy allow freedom to "consenting adults" to pursue whatever sexual adventures their fantasies propose? Does society have any stake in the institution of marriage and the family?

One of the personal and social consequences of the failure to submit to God's plan for marriage has been the epidemic of venereal diseases in the last half of the twentieth century. The venereal diseases are infectious diseases which are transmitted almost exclusively through sexual contact.[9] There was a gradual decline in the widespread incidence of syphilis and gonorrhea in the 1940s with the discovery of the effectiveness of antibiotic medicines. Although the venereal diseases were relatively dormant for several decades, they have now become a major public health problem again. The increase in the incidence of VD to epidemic proportions has coincided with the development and use of more effective birth control agents in the 1960s. This has helped create a climate that Malcolm Muggeridge characterized as America's commitment to the right of "coitus non-interruptus."

The sex-without-marriage revolt is reflected in the epidemic statistics on venereal disease. If all sexual relationships were reserved for the marriage relationship, VD would be a rare disease. But the incidence of gonorrhea has more than doubled in the past ten years in the United States. In the 1970s, there were more reported cases of venereal diseases than of all other infectious diseases combined, according to the United States Public Health Service.[10] And this shocking fact has been documented, even though many cases of VD go unreported and are not represented by the statistics. In America, alone, the rising incidence of gonorrhea is estimated to be about 7,000 new cases every day. Worldwide, there are approximately 100,000,000 new cases of gonorrhea reported annually, according to the World Health Organization. Virtually the only way of catching VD is by having sexual relations with a person infected with the disease. For this reason, the current American and worldwide epidemic of venereal disease clearly reflects the increasing sexual promiscuity of recent decades.[11]

TOO LITTLE TOO LATE. In a Christian perspective our secular response to the VD epidemic seems to be tragically naive. We are urged through a morass of "public service announcements" to know the "danger signs" of VD. We are told that periodic examinations are essential "when you are in doubt." The public is advised that VD may be quickly and discreetly treated with optimum success. But never once has any media blurb dared to raise a standard against the root cause of our epidemic—rampant

promiscuity. Not once are we challenged to chastity, to conti-
nence, or heaven forbid, to self-control.

Here's what we have on network TV. We have a half hour
"comedy" in which Laverne wonders if she is pregnant or not,
punctuated by a commercial in which attractive girls say that *all*
their men wear English Leather, or they wear "nothing at all."
We are then given a twenty-second warning which in essence
says, "If you're not careful you can contract VD." Following that
we are treated to an hour of entertainment in which Dick Van
Patten of "Eight Is Enough" learns, yet again, that his children
must be granted the freedom to experiment with "alternate life
styles." Daddy is taught, once more, that imposing his archaic
values on his children is a form of overprotective manipulation.
Making his Everyman's journey through the jungle of acceptable
video moralisms, Daddy weekly is led to the "truth" that "the
times, they are a-changing," and with a benign smile, possessing
perhaps a trace of amused disfavor, he yields to the blessings of
permissiveness. This is accomplished in twenty-minute blocks
interrupted by various seductively dressed young women who
crawl all over Mercury's latest models while a jungle cat prances
(advertising executives hopefully anticipate) across our overly
stimulated libidos.[12]

In our Western democratic societies, should we simply allow
the revolt against marriage to occur as part of the protection of
individual freedoms? Or is this an area in which freedom of
action infringes on the rights of others and the general well-being
of society? What is VD's social cost in loss of human lives, in loss
of work productivity, loss of physician time, and loss of financial
resources by health insurance and government welfare dollars? It
is tremendous. The revolt against marriage is extremely costly, as
measured alone in terms of the price of VD paid by those in
revolt—and the price sometimes paid by innocent third parties.

The sexual mirage. Pornography has been defined in many
different ways. Pornography is material deliberately designed to
produce a strong arousal. Pornography is masturbation—meant
to arouse sexual interest in the absence of personal human
contact, let alone a one-to-one human relationship. Pornography
is actually a form of prostitution because it advertises and
advocates sex for sale, pleasure for a price.

In their excellent book, *Pornography: The Sexual Mirage,* psychologist Dr. John W. Drakeford and noted artist Jack Hamm make a clear distinction between legitimate art and literature which deal with the field of human sexuality, and true pornography.

The main difference between pornography and these other types of writing is that pornography is not really concerned about reality at all. It is a psychological aphrodisiac which uses literary techniques for evoking erotic imagery to bring about sexual arousal in the mind of its readers. In most of these writings, the plot and its development is in some instances cursory and incidental, and in others conspicuous by its absence.[13"]

MARRIAGE DENIAL. When Dr. Drakeford and artist Hamm conducted a detailed review of various types of pornography, they discovered a number of common anti-marriage themes in the material: (1) The portrayal of a woman who has pursued chastity as a misguided and unenlightened person who ends up losing her virginity; (2) various portrayals of incest, with the notion of eliminating normally held sexual taboos and promoting "uninhibited" sex; (3) the debasement of the church and any religious values pertaining to sexual morality; (4) the use of gutter language, which in many ways equates a man or a woman with his or her bodily functions alone; (5) the use of pornographic violence in the "bondage and discipline" material which is purchased by those interested in sadomasochism; (6) an unrealistic portrayal of "super-sexed males" as sex athletes who are physically endowed with unrealistic anatomy; (7) a mythical portrayal of seductive females as totally uninhibited nympho-maniacs; (8) visualizations of sexual activity with animals; (9) unrealistic detailed description of sexual anatomy and sexual behavior; (10) the use of eroticized versions of pseudoscientific reports and pornographic versions of imitation medical works on sexuality; and (11) masquerading pornographic materials under the name of "art."

While the pernicious purveyors of pornography proclaim: "We tell it like it is," one of the obvious defining characteristics of pornography is that every major aspect of reality associated with uninhibited sexual expression is ignored—such as venereal disease, unmarried mothers, sadistic patrons, pimps, child abuse, homicide of unborn children, and the emotional and spiritual ravages of guilt, anxiety, and emptiness that result from depersonalized and indiscriminate sexual expression.

LATENT PORNOGRAPHY. The pervasiveness of pornography in books, movies, and magazines in our society is widespread. Pornography is not limited to the "adult" bookstores or the purely "X"-rated theaters. Instead, pornography is gradually moving into the regular publications and movie houses attended by the general population. The behavioral scientist Victor B. Cline conducted a fascinating survey[14] on the movies screened during a four-week period in a moderately conservative Western city of 25,000. This city did not have any "porno" movie houses. During the four-week period, four trained observers attended the thirty-seven films shown in town. Fourteen percent of the films bore the classification of "G," 46 percent were rated "PG," 24 percent were rated "R" and only 16 percent were rated "X."

In total, there were 833 incidents of violence in these thirty-seven films, including three incidents of sexual sadism/ masochism. The raters found 566 sexual acts in the thirty-seven films which averaged about fifteen per film. In order of frequency, the following is a summary of the sexual actions or displays found in these thirty-seven motion pictures: nudity (168 depictions), kissing, embracing, body contact (90), bed scene with sexual connotations (49), in undergarments in sexual context (36), seductive exhibition of body (32), verbalizing sex interest/ intention (36), caressing another's sex organs while clothed (27), caressing another's sex organs while nude (21), undressing (34), explicit intercourse (19), suggested or implied intercourse (17), homosexual activity (11), oral/genital intercourse (7), toilet scene (5), rape (4), obscene gesture (4), masturbation (3), and sexual sadism/masochism (3).

PORNOGRAPHY AS PROPAGANDA. In what way is this porno- graphic material, in both X-rated and other movies, actually a demonstration of a humanistic revolt against God's command- ments for the institutions of marriage and the family? While humanists vociferously defend pornography in the name of "realism," we may ask the question—how representative of reality *is* pornography: Dr. Cline, who conducted this research study on the movies available in a typical American town, reported some shocking findings:

*In 60 percent of the films premarital and extra-marital sexual
relations were presented as "normal, acceptable, and desirable."
Seventy percent of the heroes or male leads were presented as
being to some degree sexually promiscuous (before and/or
outside of marriage.) Seventy-two percent of those films having a
heroine also presented her as being somewhat sexually promiscuous (before and/or outside of marriage). Only one film of
those analyzed suggested or depicted sexual relations between a
man and a woman legally married to each other. In 60-65% of
the films the hero and heroine who are not married to each other
have sexual relations. In some cases they are married to others,
in other cases not. In other words, the model of sex presented in
American cinema is almost entirely "illicit" with an almost total
rejection of the notion that sex might occur between men and
women married to each other.*

*In only 20-22 percent of the films were any of the principal
figures seen engaged in what might be termed healthy and
reasonably satisfying marriages. Another 20-27 percent of the
films presented the main characters in pathological marital situations and the remaining 50-51 percent of the films showed all the
key characters as unmarried or not essentially involved in
marriage. In other words, models of healthy marriage and marital
interaction are present in only a fairly small minority of the
films.*[15]

Tragically, pornography is rapidly becoming an accepted form
of entertainment in our society. The inevitable march from soft
to hard core pornography has already begun in the pages of our
newspapers and magazines as well as our movies and television
programs. Recently on a television program I was distressed to
see two men discussing a current film which depicted rather
openly the sexual relationship between a mother and her sixteen-
year-old son. This discussion was done without the slightest hint
of censure or disdain.

AN ESCALATING MENACE. Pornography is "marriage denying,"
and its widespread acceptance is a symptom of the ubiquitous
assault on the institution of marriage.

Frighteningly, pornography is equally "sex denying." In the
dynamics of pornography, sexual response is reduced to a
mechanistic performance which is devoid of love, emotional

endearment, mutual submission, or committed involvement. When pornography is indulged it promotes this impersonal and mechanistic approach to sexual arousal and can be destructive of the potential for meaningful marital sexual relationships.

In the final analysis, pornography is "life denying." Many experts in the field note with alarm that pornography, operating on a kind of hideous law of diminishing return, is resorting to more and more bizarre stimuli to elicit a response from customers who grow ever more jaded from the stimulation that softer pornography provided.[16] The growth of "snuff flicks" which conclude with an actual murder on film, the ever-mounting child pornographic rings, all speak to the fact that pornography is most certainly a demonic attack on the sanctity of life itself.

The marriage union, given man by God, though threatened by all these various weapons of Satan, remains a great power to destroy the attacks of the devil. To the degree that our society affirms God-ordained marriage, to the degree that it promotes it and takes every effort to exalt, protect, and preserve the institution—to that very degree our society will be delivered from the tragedy of broken homes, the fear of growing disease, and the disgusting avalanche of demeaning views of human life. God declared that life was good. He gave marriage to underwrite his good gift of life.

THE CHOICES BEFORE US

INTRODUCTION:
THE TERMS OF PEACE

Mike: In his fascinating book, *The Great Divorce,* C.S. Lewis takes Jude's statement of lost angelic beings as wandering stars and applies that as a poetic description of hell. Under Lewis' magic, hell becomes an ever-drifting apart of private existences. Hell consists of people wandering off, all in the dark, isolated from one another—alienated and alone. This hellish process (on which Lewis elaborates in extended metaphor) is really taking place in our society. We are separating from one another, from our families, our friends, and our God. The marriage relationship readily illustrates the intricate connection that should exist between our social, personal, and spiritual needs. Marriage should never begin in ignorance of the laws of our society, nor should it ever terminate without complete consideration of the impact that this would have on those who are involved in our daily lives. "No man," said John Donne, "is an island, entire to himself." And this is absolutely the truth that must be affirmed when we think about marriage and when we consider all the intricacies and problems that face marriage today.

George: Your commentary here on how separateness leads to disorder reminds me of our first section, where we described "the sexual confusion around us." But if that kind of separateness leads to disorder, then submission leads to order in life. By submitting to God, we find order for our moral life. By submitting to government, we find order for our social life. By submitting to an authority pattern in the church, we find order for our spiritual life. And by submitting to one another in marriage, we find order for our family life. But the lack of submission is an attitude which will infect all of these arenas of life at once.

Mike: We're treading on dangerous ground today. Liberation can lead to independence. Independence can lead to isolationism. Isolationism can lead to fragmentation, disorganization, and collapse. I'm afraid, not of freedom but of our inability to handle freedom. True freedom is found only in Jesus Christ. He's the one who gives freedom and unity. "By him," Paul said in Colossians, "all things hold together." The only liberty that is trustworthy and the only liberation that can really work is the liberation that Jesus Christ gives us. The freedom that we desperately need as men and women, created to be free, is freedom in Christ. And that is the freedom on which our marriage relationships will survive today.

George: In contrast to this ideal freedom which can be found in Christ, the kinds of freedom promised by humanism are really counterfeit. Don't you think, Mike, that the kind of individual autonomy asserted by the humanists actually turns out to be the opposite of God's type of submission? It seems to me that the kind of individual autonomy demanded by humanists fails to lead to fulfillment, but instead leads to the confusing conflict that tears marriages apart.

Mike: The Bible says that, left to our own devices, we will invariably choose the wrong direction. In many ways, George, the chapter you just concluded was sobering, to say the least. It was also enlightening. Although I've been very sensitive to the threats of pornography and promiscuity in our society, I never really saw them in as clear a light as you placed them when you called them enemies of the marriage relationship. It helped me a great deal to see that these insidious sins in our society are really satanic attacks on the marriage relationship. As a psychologist dealing with sexual problems and adjustment, George, you certainly face the serious challenge that these things present to our society daily. What real cure do Christians have to offer a world that seems unable to extricate itself from this downward spiral of promiscuity, pornography, and rampant venereal disease, all contributing to the demise of healthy marriage relationships?

George: It's sad to say that secular psychology alone can merely offer symptomatic relief from the fallout of the abandonment of the Christian ideal of marriage. To answer your question, Mike, complete restoration depends upon a person's total revamping of values regarding all his relationships—not only relationships with one another, but with God as well. God has clearly prescribed healthy male roles and healthy female roles. His commandments are not harmful to a person. In counseling, I have heard people complain about the restrictions within God's moral command- ments. In a sense, however, these are much like the restrictions we put on a small child when we say, "Don't play in the street." Perhaps the kid will complain about the restriction. And sure enough, it is a restriction, a boundary, a limitation on his action. But at the same time, it is a realistic prescription that conforms with the reality of the universe. If the kid runs out into the street, he could get run over. If a person violates the marriage relation- ship, he'll get hurt. If a person discards God's prescriptions for the male role and the female role, that person is running against the grain of reality and can only experience frustration.

Mike: It seems to me that when you search the New Testament, Jesus' prescription to such a sin-encumbered world as ours was to "repent and believe the gospel." When you look into one of the root meanings of the Greek word for repentance, you find that it means quite literally to change one's mind, to change one's outlook. We should make an exchange here between the values of a fallen world and the biblical, life-giving values that God offers us for the control of human sexuality. We must adopt these values in exchange for the deterministic values of humanism. We have to exchange the death-dealing views of the sexual liberationists for the godly images of what a man and woman are to be and how they are to conduct themselves in holiness and honor. We need to call our world to repentance and then define very clearly the terms of that repentance. In the case of sexual sin, we need to exchange one set of sexual values for another. We need to lay aside one view of the man-woman relationship for an entirely different one. We must do this no matter how unique it may appear to a morally confused world; there needs to be some basic repentance in our society today. The New Testament view of what a man is and what a woman is— that is clearly the way out of the sexual confusion which abounds in our world. Jesus called the world to repent and believe. He set choices before us. The Christian needs to continue to set these choices before the world today and offer the world life.

George: You are focusing our attention on a very basic choice in life, Mike. There is a common denominator in the radical feminist movement and in the revolt against marriage that we have discussed thus far. This common characteristic is shared by the revolt against the woman's role and the revolt against the man's role that we will talk about next. It is *a self-centered humanistic value system.* So when you talk about repentance, it must be complete repentance, which is a one-hundred-eighty-degree turn away from these various forms of revolt. It must be a repentance which results in an acceptance of God's will, as opposed to the falsehoods of this world.

Mike: When you say a one-hundred-eighty-degree turn, actually you're reflecting the root meaning of the Old Testament word for repentance, *shub.* This means quite literally "to turn from one direction to a new direction." It is not only a choice to accept a new outlook, it is also a choice to reject an old outlook. We must flatly reject the deadly direction of a society that is being lured into sexual liberation. One of the more seductive attitudes that is tempting our society today is the idea that the role of man and the role of woman are optional and arbitrary choices, open to an infinite number of variations. Let's consider the biblical challenge to such a seductive and ultimately destructive viewpoint.

SEVEN
OUT OF THE SHADOWS:
The Woman's Role

MEET SALLY

After a full day's work in the office—working on this book, in fact—I was driving home, mulling over in my mind some examples that might be used as illustrations of the woman's role. I drove up to our driveway, and like a typical "absent-minded professor," I was oblivious to the routine motions of parking the car in the garage, turning off the engine, getting my briefcase out of the trunk, fumbling for the house key, closing the garage door, etc. I was pondering several possible real-life examples to use for this chapter.

I greeted my wife in the kitchen and she followed me back to the bedroom closet where I hung up my coat and took off my tie for the day. Sharon had saved up a whole day's conversation to share with me. After all, you can subsist mentally at the level of our preschooler's conversation just so long before you need another adult mind to interact with. Sharon couldn't hold it in any longer. She blurted it out in exasperation: "You won't believe what Sally said today. I just can't believe it." Sally is a young expectant mother who lives on the next block. She is in her eighth month. Sharon loves to share in the excitement with other mothers as they anticipate the arrival of their babies into the family circle.

"Sally said that she's not going to quit her job when the baby comes. She's not even going to ask for a temporary leave of absence from work. As soon as she comes home from the hospital and rests up a few days, she's going right back to full-time work. She said she thought that she should start the baby out with the full-time baby-sitter as soon as the baby comes home from the hospital. When she told me that this plan was all for the baby's best, I couldn't help asking, 'Why is that?' You'll never believe Sally's answer!

"Sally insisted, 'It's better for me to go back to work right away *so the baby won't get attached to me.*' Sally thinks that this will spare the baby the unhappy experience of missing his mommy, because he will never get attached to her in the first place! Can you believe it?"

As a clinical psychologist, I hear the unusual every day in counseling sessions. But nevertheless, I have not become totally numb to shocking examples of inhumanity in family life. Yes, it was hard to believe.

I couldn't help but think: This is it! This is my opening example for our book chapter on the woman's role in Scripture and in society today. In considering the woman's role in the last quarter of the twentieth century, Sally's approach to raising her baby sets forth the modern reality of *the choices before us.*

HOME BASE

In section one, we saw that the Bible has some definitive things to say about manhood, womanhood, sexuality, marriage, and the mutual submission of men and women to one another. But these clear moral teachings from God have been rejected outright by the humanists, who want to place the individual in an autonomous position, to decide for himself what is right and what is wrong. The rhetoric used by this revolt against God's will has been based in humanism and has led to the full-blown political programs of the radical feminists and the homosexual activists. These revolts are designed to overthrow the institutions of stable marriage and family life. Now in section two we have begun to draw the stark contrast between biblical teaching and the modern disintegration of marital fidelity, which is aided and abetted by the contemporary acceptance of sexual sin under the banner of "sexual liberation."

But not every American woman is wholeheartedly embracing

the radical feminist doctrine that: "The end of the institution of marriage is a necessary condition for the liberation of women."[1] Instead of abandoning marriage for some form of sexual deviation, many women are sticking with marriage (at least having one husband at a time, perhaps in serial monogamy, if not in lifelong fidelity). But there are degrees of capitulation to humanistic self-centeredness which lead to many varieties of women's roles being lived out in modern society. Sally illustrates one example. She is married, all right, but her concept of the woman's role does not place high priority upon the domestic responsiblity to create an intimate bond of emotional nurturance and security for the baby at home. Her approach to home life is based in humanism.

Sally is but one example of the modern sexual confusion regarding womanhood. What has happened to the traditional ideal of motherhood?

MOTHERHOOD

Our culture has regarded motherhood as among the highest and most noble roles to which a woman can aspire. For centuries the privilege of caring for children has been viewed as a fulfilling and rewarding task. Because the biological functions of childbearing and nursing placed the woman in a primary child rearing role, motherhood in the family structure became critically important in meeting the needs of a child's early life.

An enduring ideal. Historically, society has gained a great degree of stability from the ideal of motherhood within the ethically acceptable confines of marriage.[2] The concept of dignified motherhood was based in Scripture's teaching. The mother role has been preserved by the concept that the father would provide the necessary material support that would enable the wife to remain at home giving primary care to the children. The first responsibility of the mother was to provide day by day, hour by hour nurturance and guidance for the children, while the father was to provide the material needs as well as cooperative and supportive collaboration in the child rearing responsibilities.

The traditional view of motherhood involved well-defined rights and responsibilities. The mother had the right to stay at home and raise the children, as well as the right to be supported in this by the father. The mother had the primary responsibility of childbearing and child rearing which took precedence over other responsibilities outside the home. Although the role of motherhood involved much hard work and stress, it also provided a great deal of fulfillment for the woman. It was the fulfillment that came from bringing another human life into the world and directing it toward maturity.

From ideal to new deal.

NOBODY'S PERFECT. Past deviations from the traditional norms of motherhood were not seen as protests against that ideal. More often than not, they were failures to live up to that ideal. The traditional concept of motherhood was not perfect. It did not adequately embrace various social realities, for example. In the case of unwed mothers, the central violation of the traditional mothering ideal was that the child would be born outside the protective environment of the family. It was felt that a child needed both a supportive father and a nurturing mother. But unfortunately, the stigma was often placed on the child. As someone has once wisely noted, "There are no illegitimate children, only illegitimate parents." In the case of mothers who aborted their children, the traditional mothering ideal was violated altogether, and though abortion was seen as repugnant, very few supportive options were given to help the distressed mother. Similar prejudices existed against women who gave their children up for adoption.

Other clear violations of traditional motherhood include such things as the continued use of contraceptives to avoid having children altogether;[3] extensive use of child-care facilities; extensive involvement of the mother outside the home during the child's preschool years; and continued failure to provide sufficient affection to a child. These are all seen as traditional violations of the motherhood role. The most extreme violations included physical abuse and neglect, incest, and murder of children. In spite of certain elements of unreasoned prejudice, the traditional beliefs of motherhood rightly schooled us against many terrible offenses.

And though the sensible, traditional beliefs about motherhood have been around for many centuries, there are frightening indications that drastic alterations in the traditional concept of motherhood are ready to shake our society.

A frontal attack. In the last quarter of the twentieth century, this long-accepted view of motherhood has been relabeled the "myth of motherhood" by radical feminists.[4] The traditional view of motherhood is being singled out for sharp criticism by humanists who do not subscribe to the values of family life.[5] Emphasizing materialism and self-centered values, humanists have sparked the "anti-child" and the "two paycheck" revolutions in America.[6] Countless women in our country have resorted to the most drastic means to avoid bearing children altogether. Millions have sought abortion, tubal ligation, and continuous birth control, even at the risk of serious physical harm to themselves, simply to avoid the responsibilities of motherhood. Recent statistics indicating a rise in our conception rate demonstrate, however, that abstinence is considered too drastic a measure. The unbounded pursuit by Americans of pleasure without responsibility, a creed that has given us pollution, energy crises, and inflation, now threatens the very life of the family itself.

The year of whose child? In April of 1979, the popular press publicized the statistic that one out of every four children carried by women were killed through abortion during the previous year. At least fifty-five million human lives worldwide were killed before birth in a massive revolt against motherhood which has had no precedent in all of human history.[7] One wonders why these mothers feel that their life style is so threatened by the birth of a child that they would go to such extreme measures to order its death.

The abortion rate in the United States is staggering, ever since the United States Supreme Court legalized the killing of human life in its early stages. Certainly the most wealthy nation on earth cannot plead economic reasons for killing such a number of human lives without appearing to be monstrously greedy for material objects. Instead, the mass killing of young human lives appears to be a reflection of a wholesale abandonment of the traditional values which held human life and the feminine role of motherhood in highest regard.

The missing mother.
A GROWING TREND. The traditional task of the woman with
small preschool children was the full-time care and nurture of
these children at home. In the twentieth century, we have seen a
radical change in the role of mothers. It has been a steady trend
for mothers to obtain employment outside the home.[8] In 1890
(the first year that reliable records were ever kept in the U.S.A.)
only 18 percent of females over thirteen years old, and 5 percent
of married women, were employed.[9] In 1948, only one quarter of
the mothers of school-age children were working outside the
home. By 1975, 52 percent of married women with children aged
six to seventeen years, and 37 percent of those with children
under six years, were either working or looking for work. Of
those who had jobs, more than two-thirds were working full time.
   The most recent and also the most rapid increase in the
employment of mothers has occurred in the 1970s for those
mothers of children under six years of age. In the 1970s, one-
third of all married women with children under six were in the
labor force, which was three times the rate in the late 1940s. The
vast majority of these mothers have children under age three
years. These statistics take into account only the families in which
the husband was present, and if we include the growing numbers
of single-parent homes, the proportion of mothers of young
children in the labor force is much higher, as we shall see. It is
alarming that in the growing trend of the working mother, not
only are more mothers working outside of the home, but an
increasing number of these mothers are leaving preschoolers and
infants in the care of others.
   In September 1979, six economists and sociologists released the
results of their research in a book entitled *The Subtle Revolution:
Women at Work.* The authors pointed out that currently, slightly
less than one-third of American wives are full-time homemakers,
raising children. The full-time mother is rapidly becoming the
rare exception rather than the rule. This research estimated that
eleven million more women would obtain jobs outside the home
by 1990, and the majority of these women will be mothers. In
fact, these employment experts predicted that "two of every three
American mothers will be holding a job in 1990 as a huge exodus
of women from the home to the workplace continues."[10] This

same two-thirds percentage employment was predicted for unmarried mothers.

By 1990, only one-fourth of all American mothers will devote full-time attention to motherhood.

THE ABANDONED CHILD. ". . . the number of children under age six who will have working mothers is expected to rise from a current 6.4 million to 10.5 million . . .,"[11] such that 45 percent of all preschool children will suffer the absence of their mother due to her employment outside the home.

Many mothers with outside jobs face "role overload," according to Dr. Lucia Gilbert, a psychologist at the University of Texas. Some of these mothers of young children try to become "super moms" in order to handle the responsibilities of the outside job and mothering their preschool children at the same time. Dr. Gilbert commented, "They tell themselves, 'I'll drive a little faster and I'll buy a crock pot.[12]'"

The day-care dilemma. Single parents who need to be employed to support their children and themselves usually have little choice other than to find some kind of child-care arrangement for their preschool-aged children. In two-parent homes in which both mother and father choose to join the work force, some type of substitute child care is usually arranged. The number of these "two-paycheck" families doubled in the decade of the late 1960s to the late 1970s. But mothers in the work force are not the only ones placing an increasing demand upon child-care programs. From 1967 to 1976, the percentage of children whose mothers were *not* in the work force, who were nevertheless enrolled in preprimary child programs, increased from 12 percent to 29 percent. In each case, more and more children under the age of five years are spending less and less time in the direct care of their mothers.[13]

The recent trend to discard the traditional American motherhood role of taking care of preschool children is illustrated by the statistics on the use of day-care centers and other types of substitute nonparental care of children in the United States. In 1974, 79 percent of all five-year-olds were enrolled in preschool programs. Thirty-eight percent of the four-year-olds and 20 percent of the three-year-olds were enrolled in preschool programs across the country, and the numbers have been climbing since then. What is not reflected in these statistics is the fact that even more preschool-age children are provided care under informal cooperative arrangements with neighbors, relatives, or friends.[14] Most disturbing of all, however, is the fact that more than one million school-aged children have been estimated to have no formal care at all between the hours of school closing and parental return from work. This growing number of unsupervised young children are called the "latch-key children" who unlock their empty home themselves to wait alone for Mom or for Dad's return from work.

If the ideal circumstance is for the mother to be at home with the preschool-aged child to provide personalized care and a continuity of affectionate bonding with the child,[15] then the worst circumstance is that of the "latch-key child" who has no adult at all to provide supervision and care. Certainly, providing a day-care center environment for the child is to be preferred to total physical abandonment. Furthermore, there are a minority of parents who are so irresponsible or emotionally disturbed themselves that their child would be better off in the sane environment of a day-care center.

But what about those families in which the mother is reasonably skilled in parenting ability but chooses to work outside the home instead of caring for her preschool child? Because so many mothers of preschool-aged children who work outside the home rely on day-care centers, it is important to consider whether or not the use of these centers provides a reasonable substitute for the mothering which the child could have had at home.

The practical question arises: Could a caring mother provide better emotional care for her own child at home, as compared to the quality of day-care facilities commonly available? U.C.L.A. psychologists Carol A. Falender and Albert Mehrabian reviewed the research studies on child-care programs and offered this explanation:

Thus, children who leave emotionally unpreferred home settings to attend highly preferred day care settings are expected to benefit more than those coming from preferred home settings

to the same day care environments. Similarly, children who leave
preferred home environments to attend unpreferred day-care
settings are expected to suffer more than those who attend such
settings, coming from unpreferred home environments.

Thus, the extent of problem behaviors, separation anxiety, and
long-term negative consequences on intellectual and social
development is expected to be directly proportional to the
difference in the preference for home and day care environments.[16]

So if day-care centers are likely to be detrimental for a young
child if they provide an inferior emotional environment to that
found at home, how good are the day-care centers in America?

Selma Fraiberg has published a recent study of day-care
centers in her book *Every Child's Birthright: In Defense of
Mothering.*[17] Dr. Fraiberg concludes that day-care centers are
usually not emotionally healthy places for young children to
spend large amounts of their time attending. Dr. Fraiberg's study
highlights certain risks of placing the child in day centers which
are too often worlds of anonymous baby-sitters, so far as the
child is concerned.

Unfortunately, only a small minority of day-care centers in
America systematically use principles of child care which have
been derived from our knowledge of the psychological needs of
young children. Too many child-care arrangements are designed
for the convenience of the parents and staff rather than having
the needs of the child as their primary concern. Typically, group
child care is accomplished by a rotating staff. This is contrary to
the psychological needs of a small child for attention from a
constant person.

Even in the rare case of "ideal" day-care programs with better
one-to-one relationships, some research suggests that the positive
features of the program may be cancelled out if the child stays
more than six hours a day.[18] Dr. Fraiberg concludes, "What we
see is a longing for mother and home. The nice teacher, 'best
friends,' the lovely toys can no longer substitute."

NO PLACE LIKE HOME. Mary Keyserling, the former director of
the Women's Bureau of the United States Department of Labor
conducted a study of day-care centers. This study found that only
1 percent of the proprietary day-care centers were "superior," 14

percent were "good," 36 percent were "fair," and 50 percent were "poor," including many which were actually harmful to the children. The nonprofit centers faired slightly better, but only 37 rated "good" or "superior," with 50 percent rated "fair" and 11 percent rated "poor." The national average (median) of day-care staff-to-child ratios are between 1:10 and 1:19. However, the recommended federal day-care staff-to-child ratio for infants is 1:3, for toddlers 1:4, and for preschoolers 1:7 to 1:10. This means that the majority of day-care programs offer, at very best, only custodial care for young children. These nurseries are not desirable "mother substitutes," nor are they quality educational programs. [19]

YOU CAN'T BUY BONDS. Some psychological research suggests the need of early human bonding between the child and mother. The consequences of failure to meet a child's need for stable human relationships in the early years can include the risk of permanent damage in the person's capacity to make adaptive human attachments in later life. [20] A child who has been deprived of intimate mothering experiences is at higher risk for disorders of aggression and impulse control. The degree of emotional impairment to the child appears to be roughly equivalent to the amount of mothering that the child lost in early years, according to Dr. Fraiberg's analysis.

ACCIDENTS WAITING TO HAPPEN. When these young preschool children spend eight to twelve hours of their waking day being cared for by busy, anonymous, and indifferent custodians, it is clear that the child's development suffers. Dr. Fraiberg warns of the risk that these children run in developing problems of nonattachment in adult life. The failure of these children to experience normal mothering in early childhood can cause problems of emotional poverty, insecurity, and psychological conflict.

The need for sustained, intimate, and affectionate human relationships in the early years is less likely to be fulfilled by child-care center substitutes than it is by the child's own mother. While nurseries may solve a mother's immediate problem of having young children and a career simultaneously, the long-range cost in abnormal child development may be a higher price than many concerned mothers wish to pay if they know the facts. [21]

It has been argued that the emotional and spiritual poverty which result from inadequate parenting directly contribute to the many problems facing children today: drug abuse, teenage suicide, juvenile delinquency, and running away.[22] When the mother turns to career rather than mothering in the preschool years, the child is often left to the typically depersonalized existence of a day-care center. In our technological society, humans have been reduced to just another number at earlier and earlier ages.

The choices before us. Does the woman have a unique role and responsibility to provide psychological order, continuity of affectionate bonding, and personalized care that characterizes the traditional motherhood ideal? Does our recognition of the past abuses of male chauvinism require that women totally abandon any uniqueness to their womanhood? Does the correction of past injustices and discriminations against women require that we homogenize women into society to such a point that they are indistinguishable from men? Or are there elements of a woman's role that should be preserved as their unique contributions to human society?

Our answers to these questions will depend upon the deliberate choice of a starting point. Shall we start with a humanistic world view that leads ultimately to the radical feminism described in chapter three? Or shall we start with the Bible's teaching? Each woman must make her own choice regarding her starting point. Will she start with the presupposition that she is her own judge in these matters? That is what the humanists teach. Or will she look to God's will, expressed in Scripture, as her starting point for understanding her role and purpose?

But before a hasty choice is made, let's take one more look at Scripture to draw out the major teachings regarding the woman's role. Then we will turn our attention to some contemporary trends in women's roles, particularly as they relate to the home and family life. We hope to leave it largely to the reader's imagination as to how these scriptural teachings need to be applied today in the complex social matrix of home, church, and work settings of women's lives.

Mike, the floor is yours. What more can be said regarding the Bible's teaching on the woman's role?

A WOMAN'S ROLE IN SCRIPTURE

Friends, Romans, and other living creatures. In order to
understand more accurately the role of women spelled out in the
New Testament, we must first look at the dominant cultures that
gave birth to the New Testament.

What was the role of woman as defined in the Greco-Roman
world and in the Jewish world of the first century? To be quite
frank, sexism was a rank sin of the ancient world. As the ancient
traveler moved westward it became less intense, but it was
nonetheless pervasive. A survey of a few popular Greek proverbs
of the first century will give you some idea of the problem.[23]
"Woman is fickle," went the familiar doggerel. "Woman is
nature's greatest misfit," said another simply. "To instruct a
woman is merely to increase the poison of a dangerous serpent."
And so it went. Demosthenes received little argument when he
proclaimed: "We have harlots for our pleasure, concubines for
daily physical use, and wives to bring up children and to be
faithful stewards in household matters." There you have it. All
women were divided into three potential groups: harlots,
concubines, and wives. And each role was for man's pleasure.
How Demosthenes would have been astounded at our disgust!
Not only was he comfortably promiscuous, but this contemptuous
attitude toward women seems to pass without question in his
thinking.

The Roman middle class, influenced by austere stoicism, was
somewhat better, as were most militaristic societies, concerning
the equality of the sexes. However, as Roman affluence grew,
the woman often became either a sex object or a beast of
burden to many of Rome's citizens.

Keeping women kosher. One might have hoped that the Jewish
community, having the clear teaching of the Old Testament
which placed women in a high position, would have treated
women better than did their Gentile neighbors. They did not.
The male chauvinism of the rabbis was notorious. "A man," said
one rabbi, "should be thankful that he is not an unbeliever,
uncivilized, a slave, or a woman." Another rabbi exclaimed:
"Happy is he whose children are males and woe to him whose
children are females!" According to one proverb, "Many women,
much witchcraft." Another rabbi lamented, "May the words of

Torah be burned, they should not be handed over to woman."
The ancient rabbis refused to teach women, and constantly
relegated them to servile positions.

Jesus: in the vanguard of liberation. In the light of this extreme,
widespread prejudice, Jesus' departure from the norm is even
more striking. Jesus radically broke with his culture regarding
the role of women. In his teaching, Jesus elevated the work of
women to a new dignity. He compared the kingdom of heaven
to a woman baking bread (Matt. 13:33). In another place he
compares the kingdom to a housewife with a lost coin (Luke
15:8). In yet another place the Lord Jesus compares his
kingdom to ten young girls (Matt. 25:1). Ever sensitive to
women's needs in a sexist world, Jesus used the plight of the
widow to illustrate truth about prayer (Luke 18:1). By such
radical measures, Jesus confronted his culture. Other rabbis in
his time never dignified the role of women with such interest and
sensitivity.

Jesus broke with tradition in other ways concerning women.
He freely initiated conversation with them, in one instance with
a Samaritan (John 4:27)! Jesus taught women without hesitation
(Luke 10:39), and on one occasion called a member of his
audience "daughter of Abraham" (Luke 13:16). "Son of
Abraham" was a common rabbinic title for a good man, but to
use the phrase to describe a woman was simply unheard of.
With all of this, Jesus was still sensitive to propriety. Some
suggest that his refusal to enter the bedchamber of Jairus'
daughter alone (Mark 5:40) was indicative of his strong sense of
propriety.

If the title can be used of anyone, Jesus was certainly a
champion of women's rights, and often decried their abuse in his
society. He was ever sensitive to the widow (Mark 12:40-44). He
refused to keep women from worshiping with men (Mark 14:6).
Jesus gladly stood up for a guilty woman, when it became
apparent that she had been abused by male authorities (John
8:1-11). Jesus often broke with Jewish taboos to help women
when even the most liberal rabbis of his day would not. He
broke Sabbath custom to heal an arthritic woman (Luke 13:10)
and talked freely with a Gentile woman before healing her
daughter (Mark 7:24-30). In Mark 5:21-43, Jesus happily

dispensed with ceremonial purity to take a dead girl by the hand and restore her to life. On the way to that encounter, Jesus allowed a suffering woman, afflicted with a female disorder that rendered her ceremonially unclean, to touch his clothing. In laying aside the cultural taboos, Jesus was able to heal the woman.

When you consider these examples, is it any wonder that many women followed him as he traveled and taught (Luke 8:2)? At his crucifixion, the women showed more boldness and fidelity than did the twelve (Mark 15:40, 41). And women were among the first witnesses to and proclaimers of his resurrection.

So radical was Jesus' challenge of traditions concerning women, that many of his disciples found it difficult to equal his toleration. In one familiar episode, apparently feeling that the Master was far too important to entertain them, the disciples sought to restrain simple mothers and children from gaining an audience with the Lord. For their blindness, the disciples were roundly rebuked. The lesson was difficult to learn, however, and the disciples still rebuked the woman who bought the costly ointment as extravagant. They also tended to doubt the resurrection report of Mary Magdalene on apparently sexist grounds.

It wasn't until Pentecost, when the Spirit of Christ entered his church, that Galatians 3:28, "There is neither male nor female; for you are all one in Christ Jesus," became a reality. After Pentecost, the disciples were fully able to spread the redemptive revolution of the gospel. Part of the revolution was the remarkable liberation of women from the repressive culture.

The early church: heirs of liberation. The early church was a remarkable and culturally anomalous institution with regard to the question of the equality of the sexes. From the very start, women played key roles in the early church. Women were present at Pentecost. The first church met in the home of a woman (Acts 12:12). Many of Paul's young churches were founded with men and women together (Acts 17:4, 12, 34). Their special mention in Paul's letters highlights the unusual nature of that fact. Even the language of the early church, while recognizing sexual distinctions, acknowledged equality. Men were "brothers" (Rom. 12:1) and women were "sisters" (Rom. 16:1).

Not only did the early church express equality in its constitution, it proclaimed it in its function. Women were not only active in charitable work (as was the well-known Dorcas of Acts 9:36), they were strategic in church planting (as was the lesser-known Lydia of Acts 16:15). Women served as deacons (Phoebe, Rom. 16:1) and were active in evangelism (Euodia and Syntyche, Philippians 4:2, 3: and Priscilla, active in Corinth, Ephesus, and Rome). Women served as key workers in many churches. Paul mentions six such women at Rome alone (Rom. 16:1-20).[24] The church, following the lead of her Lord, broke with sexism (as it had with slavery), radically, though nonviolently. Would that twentieth century Evangelicals would follow in their steps.

A modern dilemma: harmony or conformity? When we have such a remarkable heritage, why does so much of the world today believe that biblical Christianity advocates a form of male chauvinism? A twofold answer to that question can be given. Many advocates of biblical Christianity practice an unthinking discrimination. They are guilty of nonbiblical sexual prejudice. This should come as no surprise to anyone who is convinced of the sinful nature of even the best of people. But beyond that lamentable fact lies the reality that the world does not understand or accept the sexual roles God has assigned to both men and women. The world cannot or will not grasp the fact that equality is not identical to uniformity.

To hold to a view of the uniformity of the sexes is to deny some of the fundamental truths of human nature and to threaten the laws of God and man. The basic principle regarding the distinction of the sexes is put forward in Genesis 1:27: "So God created man in his own image, in the image of God he created him; *male and female he created them.*" Here we must acknowledge that truth about God and man is expressed in the creation of human sexuality. Human sexual differentiation is a basic element of the *"imago dei,"* the image of God.

If we consider human sexuality in its physiological and psychological function, it is clear that God has designed in male sexuality a principle of initiation and in female sexuality a principle of response. These two principles working harmoniously together express a potential for creative growth and satisfaction that beautifully illustrates the creativity and love at the core of the Godhead.

If we insist that the principle of masculine initiation and feminine response is apparent from scriptural, physiological, and psychological data, then the biblical insistence of the submission of the woman in the church and in marriage represents a logical division of labor among equals who are "joint heirs of the grace of life" (1 Peter 3:7). Functioning so as to express their God-given differences, the two equal parties experience in themselves, and express to others, the blessing of doing things God's way. They "magnify their office," as Paul would say concerning his life's calling as an apostle.

Calling all sexes. We must consider our role as male or female as a "sexual calling." As with the offices within the body of Christ, and as with gifts expressed by the body of Christ, so it is with human sexuality. Human sexuality is determined by the will of God, not man. There is equality in Christ; "We are all one in Christ Jesus." But order, authority, and a division of labor also exist in the body.

God set up "first apostles"; the Bible teaches us that there are "higher" gifts. All of this is established according to the sovereign will of God. Paul was "called to be an apostle," and the gifts of the Spirit, differing in function and in importance, are distributed by the Spirit "as he wills." So it is with human sexuality. It is a gift of God, according to his will.

Reading the big print. The principle of masculine initiation and feminine response, which God has imprinted upon human sexual behavior, expresses basic truths about God and man, especially what is involved in the "image of God." This "image" is what enables God and man to relate uniquely. It is a "point of contact."

According to Romans 1, when idolatry and sexual perversion invade a society, truth about God ("that which can be known about God") is lost. What truth about God is expressed in human sexual differences? One eternal truth suggested about God from human sexuality is his plurality. "The head of every man is Christ, the head of a woman is her husband, and the head of

Christ is God" (1 Cor. 11:3). When human sexuality is functioning properly, we are given a picture of God's creative power and his sustaining love. As submission in the church and the home is observed, we are reminded of our duty to be subject to Christ, since the woman is a perfect picture of a believer ("the glory of man," 1 Cor. 11:7). Admittedly, this is a "great mystery"; nevertheless, we can all be instructed by it.

Ring around the collar, pocketful of stereotypes. It is a great tragedy that unjust sexual discrimination has often been practiced by churches, thus confusing many as to the biblical patterns for human sexuality. Jesus has set women free from the tyranny of male chauvinism. But, as always, the freedom that Christ brings is accompanied by responsibility.

A Christian woman is responsible to fulfill her sexual calling. She is to be submissive to her own husband, if married; she is to refrain from teaching men in the church (the reasons for this were explained in chapters 4 and 5); and she is to take a leading role in the encouragement within the church of stable family units. Men have a domestic responsibility, to be sure, and if they fail at this, they are pronounced "worse than an unbeliever" (1 Tim. 5:8). But note also the general responsibilities of women in domestic life in Titus 2:3-5:

Bid the older women likewise to be reverent in behavior, not to be slanderers or slaves to drink; they are to teach what is good, and so train the young women to love their husbands and children, to be sensible, chaste, domestic, kind, and submissive to their husbands, that the Word of God may not be discredited.

Many godly women in the New Testament were not housewives (for example, Chloe of Corinth and Lydia of Philippi). Nevertheless, a responsibility to oversee domestic matters is clearly a duty ascribed by God to women. They are to "rule their households" *(oikodespotein,*[25] 1 Tim. 5:14) with authority. However this is carried out, it is to be a concern of women both in their own homes and among the families of their local assembly.

Unfortunately, due to the unrewarding nature of much housework (and a society that puts a greater premium on eliminating "ring around the collar" than promoting happiness

and humanity in the home), many women are frightened away
from the New Testament challenge to be domestic. Look again at
what domesticity is. Consider for a minute that God defines it as
a promotion of love, kindness, and sensible purity. That is what
God desires in our family unity, not merely the removal of "waxy
buildup" on our floors. Turn off the TV; these commercials are
killing us.

We already live in a society that believes that, "Cleanliness is
next to godliness." Well, in households of small children and
limited budgets, the truth is that cleanliness is often "next to
impossible." But that is not God's greatest desire for his people.
He desires well-ordered families so that all can know that he
is God. Such knowledge is best perceived in harmonious family
relationships where authority is clearly defined and well-honored,
and the sexual modeling best reflects the great theological truths
about God's very nature.

While insisting that domesticity is definitely part of a woman's
role, we should avoid the arbitrary and silly practice of labeling
certain chores "woman's work." There is nothing inherently
feminine about washing dishes or vacuuming the rug. If there is
agreement among man and wife, there is nothing wrong with a
man doing dishes or a woman mowing the lawn. (Frankly, I
would rather do the dishes!) The issue is not so much the kinds
of work done, but the level of the woman's concern for the well-
being of her home.

Getting the message. There are other very positive factors in the
woman's role. Being a "responder," the woman is very sensitive to
spiritual guidance. As in the case of Samuel's mother, Samson's
mother, or the mother of Jesus, God spoke initially to the
woman. The woman, being sensitive to another's leadership, was
open to God's direction. In the three cases mentioned above, the
Lord's leading was tested by the men and their leadership was
encouraged, but the fact remains that God made himself known
initially to the woman.

In a marriage relationship, the wife is often the source of
divine insights into decisions and directions which the couple
must make. The leadership of the male is much needed here as a
source of ratification and initiation. The woman is also very
vulnerable in this area. When Paul points out that the woman

was deceived first (1 Tim. 2), he is not laying the groundwork for punishing her female descendants. He is reminding us all of the disaster that occurred when woman stepped out of her role and began initiating family decisions after she was tempted by the serpent. Once again we can note, in a negative illustration, the fact that the woman was very open to spiritual influence. In this case the result was disastrous. Could this explain the fact that so many "Christian" cults were founded and carried on by women?

Of course, all that I've said here about Scripture's clear teachings regarding women must be understood in the greater context of the biblical instruction concerning human sexuality (see chapter one) and the doctrine of submission, as it applies to women (see chapters four and five). The full biblical revelation must be considered in order to understand the several aspects of the woman's uniqueness in creation.

POINT-COUNTERPOINT

George: Sharon and I know a young Christian couple who have two children—a four-year-old and a one-year-old. They bought a new middle-class house in a new middle-class neighborhood and drive two middle-class cars. (No, they do not have the standard middle-class dog, but does their cat count?) Now, there is nothing intrinsically wrong with being middle class. But at what price?

Well, when we first knew them, they did not yet have their younger child, and the wife worked as a schoolteacher. About the time their second child came along, they tried to get by in their middle-class comfort without the second income of the wife's teaching job. But financial pressures brought on by their level of spending forced them to make a choice. Either they could not afford to continue living in their middle-class house at their middle-class rate of spending, or the mother would have to go back to work. Their initial decision was part-time moonlighting by the dad. Then later, the mother took on one part-time job. Still later, the mother took on an additional part-time job. But the financial situation was not resolved until the mother took on yet a third part-time position. Of course, all these jobs held by the parents required a complex system of baby-sitters, day-care, and preschool arrangements for the children. The parents prided themselves that the children got over their initial crying and protesting to these baby-sitting arrangements, and learned "earlier than most kids" how to be more "independent."

As a clinical psychologist, I cannot resist pointing out the common psychological defense mechanism used here. It is called "rationalization." When a person feels threatened by his or her own actions, he often defends his ego by rationalizing that the action is "for the better" anyway. In fact, this defense mechanism had reached such serious proportions that this couple began to criticize other mothers who kept their children at home, with the rationalization that these mothers of preschool-age children were "pampering" their children and "protecting them from the real world" and somehow therefore "depriving them of the chance to develop independence." They predicted dire consequences for the child whose mother stayed with him at home until kindergarten years.

Do you notice the rhetoric of revolt creeping in? This couple had decided that their material standard of living was more important than investing time in parenting and child-care responsibilities. The parents would run themselves ragged with outside jobs, having little emotional or physical reserves of energy left for their preschool children. It was unthinkable to sell their middle-class house and move back to a mobile home or to an apartment in order to allow the mother to provide an emotionally supportive environment for the young children.

When materialistic motives crowd out human caring and responsibility, the humanistic value system has crept in to displace the Christian moral teachings regarding family life, male roles, and female roles.

Mike: As a pastor, I recognize that the forces pressuring the mother out of the home are both subtle and powerful. It is difficult to compare the modern mother with the "traditional" model when it comes to environmental factors. The modern mother is the victim of many escalating pressures within American society. There is the reality of the shrinking family. More and more parents, in response to the heightened awareness of overpopulation, are having fewer children. With skyrocketing inflation figures, it is becoming ever more difficult to operate within the standard of living that has shaped our economic expectations. This same inflationary cycle is making for smaller homes at ever higher prices. Many American families are finding it impossible to own their own homes, and the trend toward condominium and apartment living is forcing today's family into narrower living spaces than ever before.

There is also the phenomenon of the "fragmented family." It appears that increasing numbers of American families are living farther from members of the "extended family." More mothers and fathers appear to be raising children with less assistance from grandparents, aunts, uncles, and other, more distant relatives than ever before.

The net result is disturbing. Smaller family units in smaller family dwellings provide for ever more intense relationships without the "buffer" of space and the diversion of other family members. With the father out of the home, the mother usually has to cope alone. She is often without extended family assistance. And whereas her counterpart of fifty years ago may have had at least the release of open play areas for the children, modern urban mothers are often "locked" tightly into a very confined space. Thus they are forced to handle intense personal interaction for long periods of time.

Clearly, changes in our environmental situation, coupled with current population shifts and trends, will require the modern mother to make major adjustments in the parenting process. But is going out into the marketplace the only option? Is the day-care center the only possible recourse? Simple platitudes such as "the mother's place is in the home" will not be sufficient ammunition against this new matrix of psychological, sociological, and economic pressure. Creative options for the mother and the child must be considered.

All at once, the local church appears to be an enormous source of supportive relationships. This is not saying that the church must enter into the preschool market (a lucrative option, though perhaps an ethical question). However, the church provides, or should provide, those kinds of responsive relationships in which mothers and fathers may find encouragement and help in their parenting.

There are other options as well. Whereas the marketplace, with all its pressures, may not provide the support that the working mother assumes it will, there are alternatives. Volunteer work in schools, retirement homes, and hospitals may indeed provide that support. Often such work can be done with the children and in a far more flexible situation than an office job could ever provide.

George: Families could exercise more courage in facing the harsh economic realities that sometimes force a choice between accustomed material comforts and close family relationships. To keep the mother at home with her preschool children, more families could choose to sacrifice living in a single-family house to live instead in a rented apartment or trailer. More families could give up their second cars, boats, recreation vehicles, TVs, eating out, a big family dog, swimming pools, expensive vacations, new clothes, beauty parlor visits, and a host of other costly material pleasures, all of which should play second fiddle to the mothering of small children.

Mike: Clearly the rewards of motherhood are not keeping pace with the pressures on motherhood in our modern world. Emulating Jesus' example, Christians should be in the vanguard of remedial measures in this regard. The options have yet to be exhausted and the problem of the working mother and the functionally orphaned child appears to be a long-term challenge to God's plan for family life.

But the role of motherhood is not the only victim of modern confusion. Let's now turn our attention to the role of the father.

EIGHT
REFLECTING GOD'S GLORY:
The Man's Role

WHAT ARE LITTLE BOYS MADE OF?

Ten years ago, a physician referred a four-year-eleven-month-old boy to me for psychological treatment.[1] The physician reported that he was physically normal. (Although it is not his real name, I will call this boy "Craig.")

Craig lived in a family that was happily intact. It included his construction-worker father, his mother, an eight-year-old brother, and a nine-month-old baby sister. Craig's main problem was that he wanted to be a girl instead of a boy. He knew the physical difference between a boy and a girl, and he realized that he had the physical characteristics of a boy, but he insisted that he wanted to be a girl instead.

This problem was not something that surfaced overnight. We discovered that Craig had a long history of wearing little girls' dresses since he was two years old. Both at his grandmother's house and in his own home, Craig would search for women's cosmetic items such as lipstick, eyeliner, powder, and rouge, which he would proudly use on his face. Time after time, he would put on little girls' or women's clothes, and then look for the makeup items to complete his feminine appearance. He was absolutely delighted whenever he could find a lady's wig to put on his head; and if he could not find a wig, he would place a mop or a towel over his head and pretend that it was long, flowing woman's hair. Craig acted like a girl in many other ways.

When other children asked him his name, he would say his name was Cindy. He could even get into neighborhood arguments about it. "My name is Cindy."

"No, it's not, your name is Craig."

"No, my name is really Cindy. I'm not a boy, I'm a girl."

"No you're not—your mommy said you are a boy."

"No she didn't, 'cause I'm really a girl."

"Well, get lost. We don't want to play with you—you queer."

It was very sad to see Craig run home crying to his mother when the other kids rejected him so cruelly. The other kids' name-calling was wrong. And it was surprising, in a way, that Craig would persist in calling himself a girl because of the ridicule it brought him from other children. But the problem persisted.

And what is more, Craig's other actions revealed the depth of his sexual identity confusion. Craig continually used little arm gestures and body mannerisms that looked like a woman's. He would make a limp wrist whenever he moved his hands. His gait was an exaggerated "swishy" walking motion. When he talked, he projected his voice into a high pitch to mimic feminine voice inflection. And most of his talk was about female topics.

At the same time, Craig almost completely ignored all the games that boys his age would play. He would avoid playing with his brother or any other boy, no matter how passive or quiet he might be. He was extremely fearful of getting hurt by the other boys. And he continually declined to defend himself if he was assaulted by his playmates.

Craig would rather play with girls, and with one neighborhood girl, Kelly, in particular. Six-year-old Kelly lived across the street and had many nice toys in her garage: baby dolls, cribs, play sinks, and the like. Kelly had brothers, too, so the garage also contained cars and trucks, but Craig had no interest in these.

Most of the boys in the neighborhood were six, seven, and eight years old and uninterested in playing house with Kelly. But Craig was interested in playing with Kelly. At first, Kelly was excited. Now she could play "mommy" and have a boy—Craig—play "daddy" with her. The first time Craig came over to her miniature home in the garage, Kelly was excited.

"Let's play house."

"OK," said Craig, "you be the daddy, and I'll be the mommy."

Kelly sighed in mild disappointment, "OK, for a little while."

But for as long as they played together, Craig never wanted to be the daddy. Eventually, Kelly insisted that it was her turn to play "mommy."

So Craig went crying home to his mom and complained, "Kelly won't let me play the way I want to play."

Eventually, all the boys refused to play with him, and shortly thereafter, none of the girls wanted to play with him. So Craig was a sad, frustrated, and lonely little boy of nearly five years.

A PSYCHOLOGIST'S DILEMMA

I have devoted ten-years' research, supported by the National Science Foundation, the Foundation's Fund for Research in Psychiatry, and the National Institute of Mental Health, to develop new psychological assessment and treatment procedures to help boys such as Craig who are not happy with their male role.[2] These problems in accepting the complete male role in childhood suggest future problems in accepting the normal adult male role.[3] In other words, I have developed treatment procedures for these confused children in order to lessen the risk that they will follow the adult pattern of a homosexual, trans-sexual, or transvestite.[4] This is extremely important in the light of the seductive attempt of the homosexual community to aggressively exploit those like Craig whose childhoods have been clouded by sexual confusion.

But I have been repeatedly and severely criticized by homosexual activists and radical feminists for trying to prevent homosexuality, transsexuality, and transvestism.[5] These "sexual liberationists" insist that there should be no distinctive differences between boys and girls, between men and women. They insist that boys and girls should be raised exactly the same, and that if Craig wants to play exclusively with girls' dresses, toys, and activities, he should be allowed to. They argue that it is "immoral" for me, as a clinical psychologist, to help Craig learn to accept a normal male role, in which he would be able to play with either boys' or girls' toys, but be secure in his identity as a boy.

Radical feminists and homosexual activists have argued in newspapers, journal articles, radio and TV, and in letters to federal and state leaders that my treatment research to help Craig and other children like him should be stopped because there is no such thing as a "normal male role." They argue that the only two choices are "macho male chauvinism," or their position that there should be no difference between the sexes. But is this true?

If we reject "male chauvinsim" as destructive, as we have in chapter three, does this mean that there is no such thing as a normal male role that is different from a normal female role? If there is a normal male role, what is it?

Think for a moment: What is uniquely masculine?

Is repairing a Mack truck? No, although more than 99 percent of all repairs to trucks are probably made by men, it is possible for a woman to do it well.

Is it having a tattoo? No, I suppose then you only need point to another culture in which the highest mark of feminine beauty is a tattoo to dispel the notion that they are for men only.

Well, what *is* it then? What is the uniqueness of being a man?

THE TOTAL MAN

For the purposes of study, it is often convenient to speak of the different parts of a person—his physical, social, psychological, or spiritual parts. But when we come down to it, we cannot literally understand the essence of maleness by separating its various aspects. Man is a whole, and the whole man is much greater than the sum of his constitutent parts.

Can a man be a man without fathering a child? Yes. Can a man be a man without marrying a woman? Certainly. But a male who promiscuously pursues heterosexual relationships outside of marriage is diminishing his masculinity just as surely as a male who is homosexually promiscuous. A chaste man, on the other hand, can experience full masculinity without ever marrying, fathering, or engaging in sexual intercourse. The sexual identity of a man rests on much more than his physiological functions. There are moral as well as physical attributes that define a man as a man.

Historically, the male role has been understood in most cultures to embody much more than its biological reproductive function. The age-old challenge, "Be a man"[6] referred to moral ideals and responsibilities, not mere sexual behavior. The social responsibilities of father and husband as well as the spiritual responsibilities of moral leadership were all embodied in the term "man."

The traditional view of a man defined him as one who assumed sexual, moral, and social responsibility as a leader and a provider as well as one who gave strength and stability. Therefore, the traditional masculine role included financial support of wife and children. Traditionally, the male would obtain gainful employment and career stability before entering into the permanent sexual relationship of marriage. In this traditional male role, a sexual relationship was postponed in order to be expressed in the intimacy of marriage. It was intended for the procreation of children within that intimate family bond.

An American epidemic. Tragically, not all American men have been committed to the traditional male role. In fact, there appears to be a growing epidemic of rejection of the masculine roles of father and husband in American society.

It may be considered uniquely masculine to impregnate a female, in the sense that a man's having sexual relations with a woman is an ultimate masculine act—biologically, psychologically, socially, and spiritually. But true masculinity is fulfilled only if this sexual act takes place within the protective confines of the marriage relationship. The privilege of the male role in heterosexual intercourse is accompanied by the responsibilities of the man in marriage and commitment to the resulting children. This was God's design.

Tragically, the last half of the twentieth century has witnessed a wholesale rejection of the true fulfillment of masculinity by millions of American men. This revolt against the traditional male role has largely taken three forms: (1) Some men marry without considering the lifelong responsibility of supporting a wife and children. (2) Some men marry without a serious commitment to the responsible male role, even if they could support their family. (3) Other men reject the traditional responsible male role by impregnating women and subsequently abandoning both the woman and child.

Kids on the skids. Often young men and women marry before the male is capable of carrying out the social responsibility of providing material support for his wife and future children. These teenage marriages are evidence of a near total ignorance of the traditional masculine role in our society. Some of the people are so young that their state laws do not grant them full participation as adults in society. They must get special permission from their parents to engage in the legal contract of marriage. Such marriages are open to all kinds of problems. The young parent appears far too often in the national statistics regarding such problems as infant mortality, attempted suicide, family instability, divorce rates, unemployment, underemployment, welfare dependency, and single motherhood.[7]

When a teenage husband abandons the traditional masculine role of financial support, and the wife abandons the traditional feminine role of full-time motherhood, the needs of an infant born to the couple cannot adequately be met. There is unusual stress on the family unit as the immature teenagers attempt to adjust to one another. The normal adjustment problems of marriage become insurmountable because traditional masculine and feminine role definitions have been abandoned. These couples need time to mature and adjust to one another, but the demands of early infant care and basic work for survival are too great. Time that could be used to learn harmonious family roles is lost to the continuous struggle of making ends meet.

The young families are extremely unstable, and because they are so unstable, they are overrepresented in the divorce statistics. When these marriages break up, of course, the greatest loser is the child. The initial failure of the younger man to face his masculine responsibilities often results in a child being raised in a single-parent home, and a single mother being forced to struggle with financial burdens. She also often experiences guilt because the child is being raised more by professional baby-sitters than by loving parents.

The fleeing father. Until the middle of the twentieth century, the majority of Americans accepted traditional roles of men and women with regard to marriage and the family. Divorces were a scandal and relatively unknown in most families. They were considered wrong, and avoided at all cost.

A simple test to illustrate the incredible acceleration of divorce

and its inescapable impact on our daily life would be the
following:

1. If you are a parent over thirty, count how many children
   from divorced homes you knew and played with as a
   child.
2. Now count how many such children your own children
   know and play with.

Chances are your kids are three to four times more aware of
divorce and its possibility than you were. What impact will such
knowledge have on your children?

Many men and women no longer view lifetime marriage as a
desirable ideal for themselves. By 1974, there were 970,000
American divorces or reported annulments in a single year which
involved roughly 1.2 million children. In 1950, about one in
every twelve children under the age of eighteen was living in a
single-parent family. But by the year 1975, more than one in
every six children under age eighteen was living in a single-parent
family.[8]

The remarriage rate lags far behind the divorce rate, especially
in homes with children.[9] Ninety-five percent of the single-parent
homes are headed by women. Studies reveal that only 3.7 percent
of these divorced or widowed mothers remarry in a given year.
Therefore, the statistics on single-parent homes do not simply
represent a temporary transitional state that will change through
remarriage. Significant numbers of children are spending large
portions of their childhood years in homes without a father. This
is one of the serious results of a mass revolt against the male role
by American men.

The number of adults in the home who might care for a child
has decreased steadily over the past thirty years, which means
there has been a definite transition from the extended family
(including relatives other than the parents) to the nuclear family
(mother and father only). And as we have seen, the disap-
pearance of adults from the home has not been restricted to
other relatives, but tragically today involves the parents as well.

Over the past twenty-five years, there has been a dramatic
increase in the percentage of homes with only one parent present.
About one of every six children under the age of eighteen years
now lives in a single-parent home. This rate has doubled in the

last twenty-five years. The most rapid increase has been in the number of single-parent homes involving children under six years of age. At present, one of every eight infants under age three lives in a single-parent home.

The step by step disintegration of the American family is accelerating. Among single-parent mothers of school-age children, 67 percent work outside the home. Among single-parent mothers who have children under six, 54 percent work outside the home. And among single-parent mothers of children under three, 45 percent work outside the home.[10]. It becomes painfully obvious that when the father abandons the family, the mother also becomes less available to the child. Like the proverbial falling dominoes, the family structure gives way to complete collapse. The child is left a psychological orphan.

Illegitimate fathers. In 1948, there were thirty-eight illegitimate babies born in every 1000 births. By the early 1970s, the rate was 130 out of every 1000 babies born. Perhaps we should avoid using the term "illegitimate child" which unjustly stigmatizes the innocent.[11] Instead, a fairer use of the concept would be to refer to "illegitimate parents." If we have a category for the "unwed mother" and some crassly call an innocent child born out of wedlock a "bastard," what should we call the father?

Since 1970, a growing proportion of unmarried women have borne children. In the first half of the twentieth century this was quite unusual. Now the attitudes of women regarding their role in society have shifted to such an extent that society no longer restrains with any effectiveness the spread of unmarried motherhood. Women under the age of twenty-five account for over 80 percent of all illegitimate births. This fact parallels the increasing trend for women to postpone marriage until they are twenty-five years of age or older.

The rapid and striking increase in the number of children born out of wedlock over the past thirty years is a reflection of the modern abandonment of the fatherhood role. This is a wholesale desertion by the adult male in our society from the God-given responsibilities of fatherhood. There is desertion in the infidelity of divorce and in the irresponsibility of promiscuous sex. As always, those who pay dearest are our children.

As in our last chapter, I think it would be appropriate for the

psychologist to yield to the pastor as we consider the biblical view of the male role in light of a modern desertion of men from family life.

A REAL RETREAT: THE ROLE OF MEN IN SCRIPTURE

Backward, Ho! An old wag was said to have longed for the days "when men were men and women were grateful." There is enough truth in that wry observation to overcome its obvious drawbacks. The truth, unfortunately, is that there is a great masculine retreat taking place today, a retreat from responsibility and opportunity. The opportunities are clear enough. Solutions to many of the nagging problems of the twentieth-century family seem to depend on the willingness of men to assume their God-ordained duties. Their retreat from these duties is among the fundamental causes of the family crisis today. The modern male, in direct opposition to sexual responsibility, is either capitulating to the absurdities of the unisex mentality or taking up the defensive posture of unthinking chauvinism.

As is so often the case, a retreat from responsibility is in actuality a passive form of rebellion. Though the clamor of the media has drawn our attention to the women's revolution, few people have realized that there has been a steady defection of men from the time-honored roles of faithful husband, loving father, and strong leader (such as God's Word outlines the masculine duty). From the very earliest times God has voiced concern over the importance of men being men.

The Lord God took the man and put him in the garden of Eden to till it and keep it. . . . Then the Lord God said, "It is not good that the man should be alone; I will make him a helper fit for him." So out of the ground the Lord God formed every beast of the field and every bird of the air, and brought them to the man to see what he would call them; and whatever the man called every living creature, that was its name. The man gave names to all cattle, and to the birds of the air, and to every beast of the field; but for the man there was not found a helper fit for him. So the Lord God caused a deep sleep to fall upon the man, and while he slept took one of his ribs and closed up its place with flesh; and the rib which the Lord God had taken from the man

*he made into a woman and brought her to the man. Then the
man said, "This at last is bone of my bones and flesh of my flesh;
she shall be called Woman, because she was taken out of Man."
Therefore a man leaves his father and his mother and cleaves to
his wife, and they become one flesh. And the man and his wife
were both naked, and were not ashamed (Gen. 2:15-25).*

It is not the thrust of our discussion to examine the nature of
this narrative. Is it myth or history? Is it poetry or prose?
Frankly, if one holds to the view of Scripture that Jesus
espoused, it would be difficult if not impossible to deny the
historical reality of the man, Adam, and his wife, Eve. Though
the expression may be poetic, it seems that the account was to be
taken as factual. Yet the language is highly suggestive of deeper
truths than a mere explanation of the origin of woman. Indeed,
God's people, both in the Old and New Testament times, sought
broader understandings of these verses. The language, whatever
its ultimate purpose, is certainly an "exalted language." The
account is a weighty one.

Fresh from the garden. What are some of the factors here that
could instruct us concerning the biblical role of men? The fact
that the male is placed in a position of authority cannot be
denied. He is first entrusted with the mandate to care for God's
creation (vs. 15). His act of "naming" the animals speaks of his
authority over them and God's will to allow man to have that
initiative (Gen. 2:19. This has the connotation of subjugation).
Furthermore, when the woman is introduced into the picture,
Adam promptly gives her a name and establishes the ground
rules for the existence of marriage (vss. 23, 24). All of this is
clearly conducted under the approval of God.

While arguing for this, one must not be oblivious to the fact
that woman's unique creation certainly establishes her as an
equal: "bone of my bones, flesh of my flesh." "She was taken out
of man." With the help of Genesis 1:27, we know that the
woman is no less in the image of God—no less human—than the
man. This biblical statement compelled one ancient rabbi to
transcend the strong prejudice of his peers. He reasoned that,
"God did not take woman from man's heel that he might
dominate her, nor did he take her from his head, that she should

dominate him. God took woman from his side so that she might
be his companion, his equal, a helper fit for him."

ONE IS A LONELY NUMBER. We have tried to make the case
earlier, and the apostle states it boldly in 1 Corinthians 11, that
the male in authority functions as a symbol of God's authority.
In the face of this, sexual roles have almost sacramental force to
them. The theological truth proclaimed by the sexual roles are to
be preserved most carefully in the church and in the home. But
having established the authority of the male role, we must pay
close attention to God's analysis in Genesis 2:18: "It is not good
that the man should be alone."

What is meant by this? Certainly the personal anxiety of Adam
is to be considered; he was lonely. But is there more to this?
Could it be said from our experience, this side of the Garden of
Eden, that it is not good for society to exist dominated by the
masculine side alone? It is not good to have a male-dominated
society. It is not good for men to behave without the restraint of
loving companionship or the sensitivity of another perspective.
Beyond the sexual function of procreation there is the necessity
to preserve the quality of human life through the introduction of
the feminine approach. A society in which men do not allow
themselves to be affected by the opinion of sound feminine
judgment is greatly lacking. A family that is built upon the total
submergence of the feminine view point is also lacking. A
marriage that is not a cooperative venture, with the male drawing
considerable support from the female and the female drawing
considerable support from the male, is less than it could be.

"WILLING TO CARE." Male authority and female equality are
held here in an easy tension. This was before the strife of the sin
nature, before the insecurities that breed a competition between
those God intended to be partners. Within the authority pattern
set up here, there seems to be an undeniable male responsibility
to preserve a protective, nonexploitative relationship with the
woman. Because of the God-given authority vested in man, the
woman is vulnerable to male tyranny. This was avoided through
the loving respect that Adam immediately bestowed on Eve.
Adam recognized not only Eve's perfection, but his own
responsibility: "Therefore a man leaves his father and his mother
and cleaves to his wife."

Scripture recognizes the need for men to assume a protective, nonexploitative relationship with women. When Peter admonishes husbands to bestow "honor on the woman as the weaker sex" (1 Peter 3:7), he is not commenting on anything other than the general physical realities that suit the woman for the toil of childbearing, and the man for the toil of family support. The woman is in need of honor since the male has the ability to be a physical tyrant.

This protective concern shapes Paul's advice to Timothy to treat "older women like mothers, younger women like sisters, in all purity" (1 Tim. 5:1, 2). The man who thinks it fashionable, or supportive to his sagging ego, to "flirt" harmlessly (so he thinks) with other women, has abandoned his responsibility to reject an exploitative relationship with women. He is arrogant and harmful. The man who insists on harboring nonbiblical views regarding women is not keeping faith with the God who requires that men have protective, respectful concern for women.

I well remember the man who told me he was teaching his son that there were only two kinds of women in the world: the good ones and the other kind. You may "have a good time" with the one type, but, he said seriously, you marry only the good ones. I wonder if he sees any connection between male behavior and female response? What would his reaction be to someone insisting that there are only two kinds of men? The first time I heard this view it struck me as quaint and innocuous. I have later discovered that it is a common view and is shared by many believers. This hostile view of women is unbiblical and dangerous. It is a denial of the protective responsibility men should hold for the reputation and dignity of all women.

"THE DATING GAME." The realities of our culture also shape the Scriptures' concern that men behave responsibly toward women. "Each one of you [ought] to know how to take a wife for himself in holiness and honor, not in the passion of lust like heathen who do not know God" (1 Thess. 4:4, 5). Since we do live in civilizations in which the men generally take the lead in man-woman relationships, once again the woman can find herself in a vulnerable position. Thus men should behave in a tender and understanding fashion. God calls for the man to sense a responsibility to protect the woman in these areas. The world, on the other hand, invites the man to exploit the woman and press

his "advantage" to a carnal end. The world invites the woman to
compete with the man, to beat him at his own game. The only
reason a woman finds this difficult is because she has been
conditioned by a sexist society (according to our modern creeds).
The woman may accept this challenge and win, but she risks the
loss of her own femininity in the process.

The duty outlined in 1 Thessalonians 4 has certain implications
for the whole dating pattern observed in our culture. It is often a
sad fact within many Christian communities that the practice of
healthy dating is discouraged. This creates many social pressures
within a society that equates popularity and acceptance with an
active dating life. It is not yielding to worldliness to acknowledge
this, nor is it worldly for Christians to redeem the practice with
an honorable and holy approach to dating. It is an unfortunate
truth that "most men prefer total abstinence to perfect
moderation." Though Augustine intended his remarks to describe
another problem entirely, they are nonetheless applicable to the
aversion to dating within many Christian communities. The result
is a rejection of a vital socializing and stabilizing process. The
absence of this process creates a great deal of tension and
confusion.

Here again the woman is vulnerable in this situation. A man
can refrain from dating because he chooses. A woman, so it
appears, doesn't date because no one has asked her. Certainly
this needn't be the case, and a woman can certainly initiate a
dating relationship with a man. It is not contrary to Scripture,
but, liberation notwithstanding, it is still contrary to our culture.
And that is a powerful force. We buck it at our own peril.
Christian dating is part of the process through which we select
our life's partner. Since the man is the initial instigator and the
woman more often assumes a passive role at first, it falls upon
the Christian man to assume the responsibility for an active and
balanced dating life.

ENTER THE RADICAL MALE. A final male responsibility drawn
from Genesis is the duty of the husband to be loyal and faithful
to his wife. A very old, though not very common, marriage vow
requires that the husband "preserve a manly affection for his
wife." How insightful. Loyalty and affection are indeed manly
qualities. Yet many give in to the outward temptation of adultery

and promiscuity, and countless others participate in the covert practice of sexual fantasy. Though Jesus warns that it is the same as adultery, since Dear Abby recommends it, many acknowledge its propriety. As a result, the "manly affection" that one is to "preserve" deteriorates before the ridiculous plastic sex images of Charlie's Angels.

Who can deny that there is rebellion within the community of the male? It is a rebellion every bit as pernicious as radical feminism and perhaps more so since it has been a common practice for much longer. It is all the more dangerous because it isn't *radical* masculinism; unfortunately, it has become a norm.

After the fall is over. Because male and female sought to run away from their God-required responsibilities after the Fall, God imposed further edicts upon their sexual roles:

To the woman he said, "I will greatly multiply your pain in childbearing; in pain you shall bring forth children, yet your desire shall be for your husband, and he shall rule over you." And to Adam he said, "Because you have listened to the voice of your wife, and have eaten of the tree of which I commanded you, 'You shall not eat of it,' cursed is the ground because of you; in toil you shall eat of it all the days of your life; thorns and thistles it shall bring forth to you; and you shall eat the plants of the field. In the sweat of your face you shall eat bread . . ."
(Gen. 3:16-19).

Though much of what is said here (and the reasoning behind it) remains a mystery, we can note with certainty that it is part of the curse that was intended to bind men and women somewhat to the realities of life without God, in order to bring them to repentance. Modern technology is beginning to overcome some of these restraints with the threatening result that men and women are finding it easier to throw off moral restraints as well. God had worked into the natural world certain harsh realities that would help men and women remain faithful to each other, whether it was the wife's desire for the husband, or the toil that held men to the land in order to scratch out even a subsistence level of survival. Once again modern technology seems to be outstripping the modern moral capacity.

New Testament manhood. The New Testament abounds with commands that were intended to define the role of men. In several places young men are urged to show respect and avoid the natural inclinations toward selfish neglect of their responsibilities to their elders. They are counseled to resist the pressures of natural sexual urges which sin can easily translate into lust and fornication. Such misdirection can be counterproductive to personal as well as spiritual growth.

IN THE EYES OF OTHERS. As one would expect, when a man takes a wife he is bound to do so in honor and holiness. That is, he must give proper respect to the opinion of God and man in the matter. Christians today are often so used to resisting the world that the concept of propriety is most neglected. Young men are often tempted to believe that if their intentions are honorable (in spite of outward appearance), if their behavior is above reproach, then they have met God's requirements. This is not so. We are called to observe honor as well as holiness. The opinion of our community concerning our sexual behavior is important.

It is sad that propriety today appears to many Christians as a form of legalism. To take care that our good is not spoken of as an evil (Rom. 14:16) appears to many as a kind of bondage. Yet Scripture repeatedly stresses the importance of having a good reputation, even when among non-Christians (Luke 2.52; Acts 16:2; 1 Tim. 3:7). In the face of this fact, many Christians do not observe propriety. They advocate unhindered access to the apartments of the opposite sex at all hours. This availability has been greatly enhanced by most major universities' abolishment of any controls on dorm visitation. The idea of a chaperone appears nearly medieval. I have frequently observed unmarried couples, with no thought of appearances, take overnight trips together— sometimes to Christian conferences. I am certain that quite often nothing improper occurs, but what a scandalous appearance. In the light of modern permissive practices, this naivete borders on the brink of stupidity.

"IT'S A MAN'S WORLD." When a man takes a wife he is commanded to live considerately with that wife. He is to honor her and love her. Husbands are to practice leadership in the home and in the church. The failure of many husbands to express and articulate love is often blamed on the fact that it seems an unmanly thing. Have we forgotten that love is a pre-eminently masculine activity? "Greater love has no man than this, that a man lay down his life for his friends" (John 15:13). Why have we feminized the concept of love? Love is the great requirement of God from his creation. It would follow, since he made his creation sexual, that there would be both a masculine love and a feminine love. Together they fulfill the great commandment.

FROM FATHER WITH LOVE. Fathers are commanded by Scripture to give loving attention to the needs of their children. In the family, a mother prefigures the responsibility of the believer, and functions as a role model for the children. The father, of course, prefigures God himself. If a father insists on assuming the indifference of most American dads, a child grows up with a preconditioned inability to believe that God loves him. Consistent behavior of the father toward the child in love and respect, however, imbues that child with a fundamental knowledge that God loves and respects him. God expects a father to naturally convey love to his children. "If you then, who are evil, know how to give good gifts to your children, how much more will the heavenly Father give the Holy Spirit to those who ask him!" (Luke 11:13).

Fathers are forbidden to be overly harsh with their children. Unrealistic expectations often produce this kind of abuse. New data on child abuse shows that it is the planned child, not the unwanted child, who is more often the victim of abuse. This probably comes from unrealistic expectations and the desire of the parents to relieve their frustrated goals through their own children. As fathers, men are specifically instructed not to "provoke your children to wrath." Jealousy on the part of the father can be the cause of much provocative criticism. The child faces opportunities that the parent never had, and even though the father might work hard to make this so, he may also feel resentment over his own deprivation. A father may be unfairly competitive with his child when he realizes that his own youth and hope for certain achievements are gone, while his child has the future yet before him.

LEAPING THE GENERATION GAP. The older men in the church have obligations to set examples of good conduct and maturity.

They are to cultivate broad concerns for the life of the whole church. Since God has given them years of life, they should share the benefit of their experience. Likewise in the church, younger men, though lacking in experience, have fresh strong minds and bodies. If they can overcome the pitfalls of arrogance and become willingly submissive, they will provide a great resource of spiritual power and encouragement.

It has been my observation, as a pastor for several years, that young men are often oblivious to the encouragement they bring to the hearts of older believers. John was never timid in admitting his appreciation of younger Christians. "No greater joy can I have than this, to hear that my children follow the truth" (3 John 4). Young Christians often express serious doubt that they have anything to give to a more mature believer. What a mistake that is. On the other hand, older Christians often misunderstand youthful exuberance and quick verbal interaction. They see it as a form of contempt for older, less glib but more stable opinions. Older Christians are often sadly blind to the great respect in which they are held by younger brothers and sisters in Christ. The older brother often sits quietly under a self-imposed silence, wrongly assuming a younger Christian isn't eager to hear his thoughts.

During the ten years I have worked in a university setting, I have seen literally thousands of young believers course through our fellowship. They long for the counsel, fellowship, and leadership of older believers. They are often eager for fathers and mothers in the Lord, having been rejected by earthly families for their faith in Christ. I mark it a minor tragedy that older Christians often place themselves instantly on the defensive when faced with the prospect of fellowship with younger believers. The Bible demands that older believers not rebel against their God-given mandate to be involved with younger believers. Older women, Paul instructs Titus, should encourage the young women (Titus 2:3, 4). That Paul himself practiced such concern is clear in his own fatherly interest in Timothy (1 Tim. 1:2, 18). The church could well encourage this by having fewer "departments" and more corporate fellowship, so that different age groups may learn to care for one another in intimate and personally satisfying ways.

Most wanted men. Certainly with respect to the role of the man in our society, there is a great failure of nerve. This is doubly tragic when such a failure strikes the Christian community. And it most certainly has. It is common for leadership in the church and the home to be surrendered to reluctant wives, because the man has decided that the demands of career or recreation take precedent. One source of weakness in the church is the fact that men are not yielding to God's call to take leadership. The great potential was outlined by John and is still offered to that community of men who will willingly resume their God-given duties as loving leaders.

I am writing to you, fathers, because you know him who is from the beginning. I am writing to you, young men, because you have overcome the evil one. I write to you, children, because you know the Father. I write to you, fathers, because you know him who is from the beginning. I write to you, young men, because you are strong, and the word of God abides in you, and you have overcome the evil one (1 John 2:13, 14).

POINT-COUNTERPOINT

Mike: George, before we begin the dialogue on this chapter, I'm curious, whatever happened to your patient Craig?

George: Craig was the first boy we helped in our treatment program. Before Craig's case, we had no guidelines for treating such a child. As we worked with Craig's parents, we recognized that the boy's dissatisfaction with his male role reflected some serious problems within his home. To make a long story short, it took us about ten months to help the family learn to encourage Craig to accept himself as a boy.

Mike: How were you able to do that, George?

George: We encouraged Craig to play out the role of a father or to pretend to be like his older brother. In the process, we found that when a child is encouraged to behave in an appropriately masculine way, he starts thinking of himself more appropriately as a man.

Mike: "As a man thinketh, so is he."

George: Precisely! Or as a psychologist might say, "Behavioral change precedes an identity change." Instead of sitting down with the boy and simply talking him into being a boy (as though we could do this through some magic words), we work intensively with his family. We used the role models of the family to help Craig behave like a boy. Craig's father was very remote from the boy. He had to be encouraged to play with Craig in a nonthreatening way and spend more time with him so that his son could feel better about his relationship with his dad. Craig's father was his most immediate source for learning what masculinity was all about. By feeling better about his relationship with his father, Craig began feeling better about his own masculinity.

Mike: How long was it before you noticed any significant change in the way Craig thought about himself?

George: One day, after about ten months of therapy, Craig, now almost six, walked into our clinic playroom while we were watching him from behind a one-way mirror. Boys' as well as girls' toys were on a table in the room. Alone in the room, Craig walked up to the table and said aloud, "These are boys' toys and these are girls' toys. I'm a boy so I'm going to play with the boys' toys."

Mike: Did Craig continue to improve?

George: We have kept close tabs on Craig for the past ten years. He is now fifteen years old. Other psychologists evaluate him every few years and report back to us. Craig now has a masculine identity indistinguishable from that of any other fifteen-year-old. He has aspirations of growing up, getting married, and having children. An interesting footnote to this case is the fact that this was a Christian family. The mother learned about our clinic on a local TV talk show. She had been praying that she could find help for her boy. She realized that both she and her husband had to do something about this problem. The first day she came into our clinic, she said, "I think your program is an answer to prayer. I've been praying for a solution." Indirectly, she was asking us to help her husband. She wanted him to be more interested in their children's development. She wanted him to take more of a leadership role in her family life, but she felt uncomfortable telling him that he needed to do this. It would be easier for her to come into a counseling situation and have the counselor speak to the father. In a real sense, God was able to work through us to help the parents minister to their own son.

Mike: What's exciting to me about your story is not just that it had a happy ending, but that there is definite hope in Christ for all kinds of problems. In our day and age, people are referring to sexual problems as incurable, as if they were totally determined situations. There's a strong sense of hopelessness that pervades our society's view of sexual difficulties. You mentioned that the Lord used your particular research to provide an answer to this woman's prayer. We can see how a Christian can offer a viable alternative to this deterministic nightmare of contemporary thinking about human sexuality.

George: As it turns out, research on the childhood histories of those who have sexual identity problems shows that a vast majority of them are very similar to Craig. Often the father is either absent or psychologically remote from the family, and this contributes to sexual confusion. The absence of a father is certainly not in God's pattern for the appropriate environment for human sexual development.

Mike: George, this gets us back to the fact that the desertion of the father and mother from their God-given roles as man and woman, as husband and wife, as mother and father, is tantamount to sexual desertion of a child. I would imagine any return to normal sexual roles is going to require a painful readjustment in many contemporary parents' life styles. I wonder if they would be willing to make such sacrifice even for their children.

George: I'm afraid you're right, Mike. Hard choices need to be made by parents for their children's sake. But the problem is compounded when the parents themselves have to work through the results of their own confused family background. They have to make hard choices for themselves as well as for their children. They need to abandon their own improper views of ideal family life and accept the clear biblical pattern of a family life that pleases God.

Mike: Amid all the modern examples of family failure, it is certainly easy to become extremely disoriented in terms of ideal family relationships.

George: I've seen examples of that in my clinical experience. I've talked with a lot of homosexuals who are so emotionally confused and spiritually blind that they see a world of males only as the best of all possible worlds. Even though this fantasy may have resulted, in part, from a lack of proper family guidance, God's guidance is still available. Mike, your treatment of that passage in Genesis 2 underscores the psychological truth that proper sexual balance in a family is the most conducive atmosphere for the sexual development of a child. In a sense, the absence of one or the other sexual perspective was never the intention of God.

Mike: I think that's definitely the case. When we look back at the initial creation account in the first chapter of Genesis, we read that "God created man, male and female, in the image of God." Then Genesis 2 may be seen as offering a different perspective on the same creation story. The fact is, according to Genesis 1 and 2, man is not completely man without feminine influence on his development. Likewise, a woman is not completely a woman without masculine impact on her development. It is not good for man to be alone. It is not good for a male perspective to be dominant and a female perspective to be all but absent.

George: You don't mean to imply, Mike, that a man cannot be a man unless he's married, do you?

Mike: Not at all. There are many channels, other than the marriage relationship, through which a feminine perspective can meet and interact with a man's perspective. There is, for example, the impact of a man's mother, or his sister, or any myriad of feminine acquaintances throughout his life, on his development. It is simply not good for man to try to exist, or even to fantasize about an existence that is totally masculine . It is not good for a man to totally steel himself against any feminine perspective. Misogyny is a violation of God's proclamation at creation that it was not good for man to be alone. A totally masculine society would be, according to the biblical data, a subhuman society. Likewise, a totally feminine society would be a subhuman society.

So the hostile, anti-feminine perspective of many homosexual communities is subhuman, and the hostile, anti-male attitudes of many radical feminists are subhuman.

George: What you're saying, Mike, also points out why a vacuum is created when a father abandons his family, either physically or psychologically—through unreasonable employment demands, the dictates of self-interests, or simple indifference.

Mike: That's true. I was interested in your remarks at the beginning of this chapter, particularly because you seemed to say that the working mother in our society is so often the single culprit in any discussion on parental abandonment. But it is in reality more a male crime than a female crime. The fact is, male abandonment of the masculine role may be driving more women into the marketplace at the expense of their motherhood role.

George: When we think about the man's responsibility in this matter, we are brought back to the point that I made about true masculinity being a responsible masculinity. This is contrary to the *Playboy* platitudes of today that falsely preach the doctrine that the most masculine act is unrestrained intercourse. This view would have us believe that we could separate a biological event from its social and moral impact on our lives. True masculinity requires the acceptance of a myriad of interrelated biological, psychological, spiritual, and social responsibilities attending the male role in all sexual expression. Infidelity might be considered by some as the ultimate "macho" life style, but in a real sense, such behavior is pseudo-masculinity, counterfeit masculinity. It is not true masculinity because it is not responsible masculinity.

Mike: George, the Bible often says that "God requires a man to be faithful." This also has a sexual application. It is to be translated into leadership, responsibility, protective love, and respect on the part of husband, sons, and brothers toward all women. It becomes very clear how the glory of God the Father is to be wonderfully reflected in true masculine behavior.

EPILOGUE
A DEFENSE WITHOUT APOLOGY

PLAYING OUT YOUR OPTIONS

Perhaps we could blame the Greeks for the ambiguity in the title to this, our last section, but it really isn't their fault. True, the word "apology" was their invention, but to them it meant "to speak in defense." How Mr. Webster could account for this word's transmutation into the English language as, among other things, "an admission of error," "an expression of regret," (or, worse yet) "a poor substitute," is anyone's guess. So, to close this book with a defense is in no way an "admission of error," or "an expression of regret." Hopefully neither will it prove to be a "poor substitute."

In truth, our world has fallen on such hard times that it appears that anyone adopting a traditional moral view of reality had better be ready to defend that particular view. So, before we close, let this epilogue be our brief defense for daring to suggest that biblical morality is the only cure to the moral evils of our age. We make this "defense without apology," with the understanding that the best defense is still a good offense.

If at first you don't succeed. The human race has yet to produce a moral system superior to the one based on the divinely revealed Judeo-Christian Scriptures. It never will. It is equally certain that it will never stop trying.

As a case in point, consider our own culture. Western culture, born and nurtured within the protective moorings of the Bible and the reasonable atmosphere of Christian philosophy, at least since the Renaissance, has sought alternatives to biblical morality. As if frustrated by its failure to create positive options, our civilization, especially in the last two or three hundred years, has been more successful in producing vicious attacks on the Bible itself.

If Scripture, as the basis of morality, were thoroughly discredited in the eyes of men, then scriptural morality itself would perish. This destructive strategy has been very effective, if not productive. In addition to these attacks, numerous alternative moral starting points have been proposed in place of the Bible. Consequently, the Bible has become, to many, a completely unreliable guide to moral behavior.

In the last two centuries, with alarming and accelerating frequency, various moral systems have risen to vie with the morality of the Bible for the hearts and minds of men. The results have been disastrous. It is important, as we conclude our defense of a biblical view of human sexuality, to realize that historically every alternative to biblically based morality has failed. Not only has each failed, but cumulatively, they have had a disastrous global impact on the well-being of human life. Though many books could be written on this fact alone, and indeed many have been written, let us consider briefly why this general observation is valid. We should ask ourselves how and why the various alternatives to biblical morality have failed us in the nineteenth and twentieth centuries.

For the sake of a general discussion, it is safe enough to say that contemporary challenges to a morality based on Scripture fall in either one of two basic categories. There are those alternatives to a biblical morality which fall under the general heading of "natural moral systems." These alternative systems are said to rest on "scientific" observation, or empirical data alone. Ironically, many proponents of such systems, while insisting on limiting data to the empirical alone, erect as their "highest good" decidedly nonempirical, subjective, and sometimes quite arbitrary qualities such as love, loyalty, etc.

A second general heading would be "humanistic moral systems." Advocates for these systems argue that personal well-being, or personal fulfillment, lies at the base of what is to be considered a moral act.

Doing what comes naturally. Natural moral systems appear to have their genesis in the early nineteenth century's fascination with all things scientific. By the middle of that century men like Herbert Spencer were eagerly applying the Darwinian hypothesis of natural selection, which they happily called an "inviolate law of nature," to ethics and human moral behavior. This "Social Darwinism" became a favorite among the late nineteenth century robber barons in England and America. Men such as multi-millionaire "Gentleman" Jim Fisk, profited off the bankruptcy of thousands and still said, "God gave me my money." Such wicked men quickly agreed with the contention that possessing great wealth was ample proof of fitness and even of superiority. They conveniently overlooked the fact that survival does not always imply moral fitness. By their narrow standards, the cockroach would be considered the superior species of our planet, the sledge hammer superior to the digital watch, and, God forbid, the Beatles superior to Bach.

Other naturalistic systems emerged alongside social Darwinism, and in a relative manner proved themselves to be more fit. Various forms of utilitarian and pragmatic value systems offered differing practical tests for what was and what was not moral. Often the "good" rested on rather arbitrary standards or upon strictly physical criteria such as overcoming suffering. The implicit myopia of such systems lies in the fact that through a brutal procrustean method, advocates of utilitarianism tended to disregard any suffering other than physical suffering, and any needs other than physical needs. This tended all too quickly to reduce man to his lowest common denominator.

It is not surprising that such views found a home most quickly among the emerging classes of the newly rich in the nineteenth century. It provided them with a sort of rationale for their lately won affluence; a fresh opportunity to follow the age-old practice of *noblesse oblige*. Meeting physical needs is always an easy substitute for solving more complex moral problems. Any consideration of more refined personal needs among the masses was considered unnecessary, as such people would lack the more refined sensitivities of the middle and upper classes. The seeds of arrogance and condescension lie deep within the moral systems forged in the furnaces of utilitarianism and pragmatism.

On the darker side, natural moral systems tended to lay the groundwork for moral skepticism, and moral skepticism moved quickly to moral cynicism. To the utilitarian, morality was seen, not as an independent absolute, but as the desired end of a given situation. It would follow, pragmatically, that if the "ends" are all there are to the issue of human moral behavior, then, of course, the ends justify the means.

It is easy to see why men like Marx saw the old morality only as a way in which the rich further enslaved the poor. Therefore, Marx would define his morality as that which promoted a classless society. Marx naively held for the good of a classless society and seldom expressed doubt about the possibility of such a historical anomaly. Marxism all too easily became a convenient weapon for the ruthless and the violent. His "classless society" became Lenin's endless revolution and ultimately Stalin's "State."

Another German, Nietzsche, while no less cynical than Marx when it came to his view of traditional morality, proved to be somewhat more worldly wise in defining moral behavior in an amoral world. Traditional morality, in the eyes of Nietzsche, was, pure and simple, the way in which the weak enslaved the strong. Far from seeing the meek as worthy heirs of the earth, Nietzsche admired the "superman," that one who could force his will on others and make sense out of the moral insanity of a universe in which God had died.

Brick by brick, in attempting to replace biblical morality, the naturalistic systems laid the foundations of modern totalitarianism. The good of "all" replaced the worth and the dignity of "each." The "all" became the "state." In reality, the totalitarian state is nothing more than a tool for the few who gain control of the apparatus of power. Tragically, moral skepticism, hidden in a rhetoric that extolls the will of the masses, becomes an easy comrade to the base self-interests of a few.

Naturalistic systems were effective in undermining the credibility of Christian morality in the eyes of many through serious attacks on their reliability of Scripture and biblical authority. The result of their labors, however, appears to be those godless political monoliths which threaten to devour Western civilization in the twentieth century. It is possible that they will be stopped by nothing short of the direct intervention by God into human history.

The test that Jesus gave to judge moral systems should, by now at least, prove to be the undoing of the naturalist: "By their fruits ye shall know them." Most see this as a warning more than a promise; it may, in reality, prove to be a curse. Because Christians have failed to fully understand and defend biblical morality, Western civilization has been forced to realize the evils of naturalism only after swallowing much of its bitter fruit. Whether the dose has been fatal remains to be seen.

Failure to reject a moral system after it produces evil fruit is folly. Leon Trotsky provides us with a graphic illustration. Writing from Mexico, the aging Marxist insisted that Bolshevism was good, but that Stalin had betrayed the revolution. Surrounded by fellow Communists who ultimately betrayed him, Trotsky wrote:

Stalin took possession of power, not with the aid of personal qualities, but with the aid of an impersonal machine (the Communist Party forged by Lenin). And it was not he who created the machine, but the machine that created him. That Machine, with its force and its authority, was the product of the prolonged and heroic struggle of the Bolshevik Party, which itself grew out of (noble) ideas. . . . The Machine had grown out of ideas. Stalin's first qualification was a contemptuous attitude toward ideas. The idea had. . . .[1]

Trotsky never finished his defense of the good ideas of Communism, because at that very moment, in the midst of that very sentence, an agent of the Soviet Union carried out Stalin's directive by burying an axe in Trotsky's head. You cannot divorce the evil from the system that produced it, if indeed it is a fruit of that system. The fruit of a natural-based morality, like sin itself, is death.

It might well be asked, if a system is to be judged by its fruits, how do we account for the failure of Christianity to hold the modern mind? How do we account for the fact that Christianity has been so vulnerable to naturalistic and humanistic deviations from its most cherished values? The answer is simply that

Western civilization has refused to acknowledge true Christian faith, and often what passed for "Christianity" was in reality false teaching. Robert E. Speer put it forth nicely:

> *Christianity began as a set of historic facts and their necessary valuation and interpretation. Any other Christianity is unauthentic. And it was and is this authentic Christianity which alone has been able to produce the social, moral, and spiritual fruitage by which the tree has been judged and proved.*[2]

To err is human(istic). The so-called "free world" has, to a large degree, recoiled from the inevitable insanity of moral systems based on natural observation alone. However, a return to a morality based on the revelation of God's will and God's nature still seems repugnant to many. In the midst of this gigantic "failure of nerve," there emerges a compromise: enter the eclectic morality of humanism. The humanistic systems are the "other options" to biblical morality.

Modern humanism was forged in the fires of reaction. When the naturalist said that God was no longer in his heaven, the humanist was pleased, but the cynical, materialistic conclusions of the naturalist were not so pleasant to him.

Spiritual values, those nonempirically determined "goods" of life, are important to humanistic systems. But, rather than defending them as springing from the nature and will of a spiritual and good God, in whose image man has been created, the humanist chooses to argue for these "goods" in a confusing patchwork of eclecticism, existentialism, and irrationalism.

For example, the humanist says of morality that there are no absolutes (absolutes are, apparently, too godly or too impersonal). All at once a Joseph Fletcher may suggest cutting through the ambiguities of conflicting moral absolutes by always doing the "loving thing." Dr. Fletcher, indeed, says this rather absolutely. Other humanists, impressed by the easy spirituality of this tender phrase, "do the loving thing," gladly overlook his "minor" internal inconsistency, and applaud Dr. Fletcher loudly, if somewhat illogically.

Of course, the problem with such an absolutely decreed good, is that the "loving thing" may alter in each and every situation.

Fletcher defines love in a completely subjective manner. Nonetheless, it is good to always do "it," whatever "it" is.

Unfortunately, love is then left to the perception or misperception of the individual. Charles Manson remains, I am told, quite confident that he did the "loving thing" and that he is still a loving person. Love becomes what love wants to be. In the wake of this creed, promiscuity becomes love, abortion becomes love, divorce becomes loving, lies are love, unconsciousness becomes bliss, and morality falls into total anarchy.

The humanistic systems of morality have their cynics also. Cynics like Camus fight against evil for no reason, since, after all, there is no reason. But, by and large, such cynicism finds no place in either the mind or heart of men. Morality based on absurdity has proven to be the greatest of all absurdities. Humanism, invented as a compromise, offers no recourse. It is a paper tiger ready to be swept away either by total permissiveness or a fierce backlash of oppression. Humanistic-based morality is blasphemy to the Christian and ultimately sheer foolishness to the world.

The greatest question of the twentieth century is not "What is truth?" but rather, "How long can we live without truth?" How long will our minds tolerate this absence of absolutes? Are we doomed to fall victims of the depersonalizing and dehumanizing of moral systems that refuse to recognize the value of human life, systems that are mere weapons in the hands of either tyrants or fools?

Paradoxically, the solution to such a cosmic dilemma rests in the familiarly clear and consistent witness of the Bible. Its basic truths, written in man's heart since the Garden of Eden, printed on the universe at creation; its ultimate truths, revealed first at Sinai and finally at Calvary, remain the sure guide to the will of God for human moral behavior. As this guide, the Bible also remains the only path to personal and societal salvation, since true moral behavior and true moral concern lead infallibly to the source of God's Word and God's morality in Jesus Christ.

OPTIONAL ILLUSIONS

"All well and good," says a disgruntled reader. "But what has this rather abstract philosophical discussion to do with sexuality? I bought this book for information about sexual behavior, not for intellectual history." There's the rub. You cannot effectively discuss any moral question without anchoring that question in the broader questions of God's will and the nature of truth.

Dividing to conquer. The tendency of the modern mind, having set itself adrift from any integrative whole, is to be content with dividing reality into more and more manageable "chunks." Taking each "chunk" as a truth in itself, and disregarding its relationship to all truth, the modern mind insulates itself against all questions of ultimate responsibility and meaning. Doubting any meaning of the whole, it zealously seeks to maintain a relative meaning for each fragment.

We are fragmenting reality and divesting ourselves of any responsibility to know and honor the bigger picture. So we are an age of specialists. Blithely ignorant of the specialties of others, we become like the fabled expert "who sought to know more and more about less and less, until he knew all about nothing."

More seriously, we become like Hitler's death camp doctors, unwilling to address broader questions of morality. They accepted the "realities" of life, and unflinchingly experimented, for the sake of "science," on human beings labeled "nonpersons" without getting "bogged down" in the morality of it all. Like the hospital administrator who avoided the morality of the abortion question by saying he was only doing "what the law allowed"; like the "Christian" psychologist in a "Christian" seminary who refused to affirm or deny the bodily resurrection of Christ since it was a theological, not a psychological question. Modern men run from the brink of decision. To quote Joe Louis: "You can run but you can't hide."

The modern approach to all problems is to divide and conquer. But what is being divided? And who is being conquered? Our public schools refuse to connect education with morality. Our universities are on their way to becoming "diversities," next stop—chaos. Our jobs are departmentalized, moral decisions are divided into unrelated segments (so that we will vote for a man who refuses to oppose immoral behavior as long as he can "whip inflation now"), and as a result our personal lives disintegrate before our eyes. We lose touch with ourselves, our loved ones, and finally our sanity. It's all "slip slidin' away."

Only news that fits. This disintegration of truth, masquerading as knowledge, creates a formidable barrier against modern minds accepting biblical solutions. The Bible views life and morality holistically. Our actions and our attitudes do not exist in a vacuum. Part of the biblical definition of man involves accountability in all that he does. The Bible insists that our actions as well as our attitudes matter; they must be appropriate to the world God has made. Because the Bible dares to integrate truth for the whole person, it is philosophically estranged from that mind bent on isolated autonomy. The Bible seems a hopeless anachronism to the "experts." It is too general and too categorical to be seriously considered by the sophisticated technicians of our day.

A friendly critic of our book lamented that he wasn't sure just what we were up to. Was this to be a book about personal therapy or social involvement? Did we want to talk about sexual perversion or proper sexual roles? How frustrating our answer must have been: yes, to all of the above. Can you talk about proper personal therapy without considering its societal impact? Can you adequately consider the issues of healthy sexual roles without considering the blight of homosexuality?

The world around us would prefer to try to do this. The man or woman failing at parenthood would prefer not to deal with the potential problems such failure might produce for their children in terms of a distorted sexual image that child might develop about itself. The counselor may prefer to think only about the well-being of his client, without considering the impact of such "well-being" on family or friends. Such "well-being" might involve divorce, promiscuity, or any number of immoral things, but as long as it's removed from the single question before him, the counselor may be content to let it remain a moot point.

By dividing reality into "chunks," we create an illusion of understanding our options more clearly. But often those so-called options are immoral. To allow ourselves to think that we have such options is, in fact, a mirage, and a deadly one. It is an optional illusion.

NO OPTIONS AT ALL

The moral blight of our age goes far beyond the questions of human sexuality. But any sane discussion of human sexuality must rest in the security of that divinely based moral system of the Word of God. In this book we have attempted to do this without apology. We began by insisting that the Bible had something to say. We close the book with that same confident assertion.

We have considered the reasons for many of the things that the Bible says regarding human sexuality, and we have pointed out many of the dead ends that are even now being pursued by a society that is apparently turning a deaf ear to the moral warnings of Scripture. Hopefully, we have helped to establish more clearly, for anyone who cares to listen, that the Bible indeed has something to say.

At the end of a decade that has seen Vietnam and Watergate, a decade of wholesale abortion, rising homosexuality, family collapse, and the brainwashing techniques of the cult explosion—after a decade of sexual eclipse—one can only wonder what harsher voices God has prepared for a nation that still fails to heed the clear counsel of Scripture. It is a still, small voice that calls to us yet: "Come now, let us reason together, says the Lord: though your sins are like scarlet, they shall be as white as snow; though they are red like crimson, they shall become like wool."

FOOTNOTES

CHAPTER ONE

1. The Gallup Poll for May, 1978, showed this fact to be the same as a similar poll taken in 1952. Though the impact of "institutional" religion seems to be lessening in the last thirty years, over the long haul there has been a steady increase in religious interest in the United States.

2. Presented at the eighty-second commencement Trinity Evangelical Divinity School, Arnold T. Olson Chapel, May, 1979, Deerfield, Illinois.

3. We all too quietly allow the continued acceleration of secularism in our public schools. We do this often in spite of many existing state laws such as those in Florida that require public school teachers to "inculcate by precept and by example *every* Christian virtue" (Florida Statutes, ch. 231.09, Sect. 2).

4. It should be pointed out that the severe Old Testament penalties for sexual perversion must not be viewed as either prescriptive for every society nor indicative of a lack of compassion in ancient Israel itself. Old Testament law has either an eternal, moral lesson extending from Israel to all nations, or it has a religious, ceremonial objective that prefigures the work of Christ; or it has a specific historical, geopolitical focus relating solely to the realities of ancient Israel's unique position among the nations.

   The harsh penalties against sexual perversion recorded in the Old Testament were part of an intense effort to keep Israel free from the influence of the corrupt practices of the nations around her, as well as to secure the intentions of God to preserve his law and ultimately bring forth his chosen Redeemer. The penalties also ceremonially depicted the purity of God and the truth that the "wages of sin is death."

The penalties against sexual perversion in the Old Testament reflect ceremonial and political realities unique to ancient Israel. To conclude from these passages that God intends the execution of sexual deviants in every society, is to misunderstand both the intention of the Old Testament law and the power of the New Testament gospel.

5. John Murray, *Principles of Conduct,* (Grand Rapids: Wm. B. Eerdmans), p. 28.

6. The word, *dabāk*, is used figuratively "of loyalty, (and) affection . . . with the idea of physical proximity retained" (Brown, Driver, *Briggs Hebrew and English Lexicon*, p. 179).

CHAPTER TWO

1. John W. Drakeford and Jack Hamm. *Pornography: The Sexual Mirage* (Nashville: Thomas Nelson, Inc.), 1973.

2. An example of the humanistic reluctance to label explicit nonmarital sexual pictures and deviant sexual literature as "pornographic" is seen in a symposium of articles on the topic "Sex Magazines and Feminism" by Lester Kirkendall, Gina Allen, Albert Ellis, and Helen Colton in *The Humanist*, 1978, 36 (6), pp. 44-51.

3. The concept of "promiscuity" has been supplanted by the notion of "sexual freedom." "Marital infidelity" is the old-fashioned way of speaking about what is now called "freedom from sexual hangups." The term "virgin" used to be a complimentary description of a moral, chaste person, but now the same person is derogatorily called, "inexperienced." By the same token, persons who succumbed to sexual acts outside of marriage used to speak of themselves as "defiled," but today the more congratulatory term "experienced" is applied to the same condition. Similarly, the traditional terminology "sexually permissive" has been replaced by the adaptive-sounding rhetoric, "free of inhibitions." The chaste virgin can now be the victim of mud-slinging—just call him "sexually inhibited"!

4. Behaviors that were previously labled "sex sin" are now renamed "sexual fulfillment."

5. The term "adultery" carries a negative moral connotation that many modern people seek to avoid. One creative renaming of extramarital

indulgence is the term "open marriage." The concept of a "closed" marriage—a faithful, chaste monogamy—now sounds as undesirable as being "closed-minded."

6. The theological concept of captivity to *sinful* practice has been replaced by the humanistic concept of "liberation" from moral sanctions. Traditional "sexual morals" have been relabeled "intolerant attitudes." Standards of "sexual purity" have been renamed "sexual represssion." What the majority would have called "sexual evil" in the nineteenth century is now called "sexual exploration" in the last quarter of the twentieth century.

7. Page 25 of *National Plan of Action Adopted at National Women's Conference, November 18-21, 1977, Houston, Texas.* Washington, D.C.: International Women's Year Commission, 1977. This publication states, "This National Plan of Action constitutes the official recommendations of The National Women's Conference, pursuant to Public Law 94-167."

8. Page 9 of *The Document: Declaration of Feminism,* 1972, Nancy Lehmann and Helen Sullinger, Box 7064, Powderhorn Station, Minneapolis, MN 55407, states, "A woman's sexuality is severely limited by the continual fear of pregnancy. To gain control over our lives we must have control over the reproductive functions of our bodies. We must have safe and effective birth control and access to free legal and safe abortions. The decision to have a child is ours and ours only—not the doctor's, the father's or anyone else's. We women are the only ones in the position to decide whether or not we can care for a child both emotionally and physically."

9. The official policy of the National Organization for Women (NOW) uses this rhetoric: "Recognizing that a woman cannot reach this potential if she is denied the basic *right* to *control of her own body,* NOW has demanded the dissemination of birth control information and contraceptives and the repeal of all laws against *abortion.*" Page 20 (italics added to point out terms used) of *Revolution: Tomorrow is NOW,* compiled by Mary Samis, Tish Sommers, Marjorie Suelzie, and Nan Wood. Published by the National Organization for Women (NOW), 1977, described on page one as the following, "This is a summary of NOW's existing resolutions and policies by issue."

10. The *National Plan of Action* cited above advocates abortion under the high sounding title of "Reproductive Freedom" on pages 25, 26. In speeches and publications by pro-abortionists, there is a repeated tendency to avoid talking about killing the unknown human life and repeated substitutions of words such as "the pregnancy" or "the woman's body" whenever the living and growing human fetus is

being talked about in terms of deliberately planning its death. This sleight-of-hand attempt to make a low view of human life sound acceptable is exposed in terms of its secular humanistic roots in the insightful analysis by Francis A. Schaeffer, D.D., and C. Everett Koop, M.D., *Whatever Happened to the Human Race?* (Old Tappan, N. J.: Revell, 1979).

11. For further discussion, see the book by Harold O. J. Brown, *Death Before Birth* (New York: Thomas Nelson, 1977).

12. For example, see A. Russell and R. Winkler, evaluation of assertive training and homosexual guidance service groups designed to improve homosexual functioning, *Journal of Consulting and Clinical Psychology,* 1977, 45 (1), 1-13; and R. C. Winkler, on "What Types of Sex-role Behavior Should Behavior Modifiers Promote?" *Journal of Applied Behavior Analysis,* 1977, 10, pp. 549-552. Also see the rebuttal by George A. Rekers, on atypical gender development and psychosocial adjustment, *Journal of Applied Behavior Analysis,* 1977, 10, pp. 559-571.

13. The first major volume derived from Kinsey's research was *Sexual Behavior in the Human Male,* by A. C. Kinsey, W. B. Pomeroy and C. E. Martin (Philadelphia: W. B. Saunders, 1948).

14. *Revolution: Tomorrow Is Now* quotes an official policy of the National Organization for Women as stating: "Our schools must be held accountable for the effective motivation and education of all students. Therefore, NOW urges educators and legislators to work with us toward the following goals: . . . the upgrading of sex education courses to include factual information on contraception and on the ecological crisis of overpopulation, and to remove all references to "ideal" or "normal," "masculine" or "feminine" etiquette, social behavior and vocations . . ." (p. 9). This source also quotes a NOW resolution that states, in part: "Realizing that each individual child has the capacity for the full range of human characteristics, the child should not be channeled into a role based on sexual stereo-types. Further research must be undertaken to discover ways to prevent sex-role channeling" (p. 15). Similarly, *The Document: Declaration of Feminism* states: "Heterosexual relationships are by their very nature oppressive to women in a male dominated society" (p. 8). The radical feminist authors of this "Declaration of Feminism" also insist: "In the past we women have been afraid to admit that marriage wasn't all it was cracked up to be because it meant we had failed. Now we know it is the institution that has failed us and *we must work to destroy it.* The end of the institution of marriage is a necessary condition for the liberation of women. Therefore, it is important for us to encourage women to leave their husbands and not to live individually with men" (pp. 11, 12).

15. The reader can see this clash of opposites in these two articles:
    (1) Darrel Smith, "Humanist Manifesto II: Five Years Later, A
    Theistic Critique," *The Humanist,* 1978, 36 (6), pp. 55-57. (2) Edwin
    H. Wilson, "Humanist Manifesto II Defended," *The Humanist,*
    1978, 36 (6), pp. 57, 58.

16. 1 Corinthians 6:9-11 warns us, ". . . do not be deceived" by those
    who use the rhetoric of revolt to give high-sounding humanistic
    terms for sinful sexual practices.

17. *Humanist Manifesto I and II* (Buffalo, New York: Prometheus
    Books, 1973).

18. Paul Kurtz in the Preface, *Humanist Manifesto I and II,* 1973.

19. Kurtz, 1973, p. 3. Paul Kurtz, editor of *The Humanist,* also pointed
    out that the *Humanist Manifesto I and II* were designed to be
    worldwide in scope and were intended ". . . as the expression of a
    quest for values and goals that we can work for and that can help
    us to take new direction" (Kurtz, 1973, p. 4).

20. *Humanist Manifesto I and II,* p. 7.

21. Humanists "believe that traditional theism, especially faith in the
    prayer-hearing God, assumed to love and care for persons, to hear
    and understand their prayers, and to be able to do something about
    them, is an unproved and outmoded faith. Salvationism, based on
    mere affirmation, still appears as harmful, diverting people with false
    hopes of heaven hereafter" (*Humanist Manifesto II,* p. 13).

22. "We believe, however, that traditional, dogmatic or authoritarian
    religions that place revelation, God, ritual, or creed above human
    needs and experience do a disservice to the human species"
    (*Humanist Manifesto II,* pp. 15, 16).

23. Quote from page 16. This passage also states: ". . . We can
    discover no divine purpose or providence for the human species.
    While there is much that we do not know, humans are responsi-
    ble for what we are or what we will become. No deity will save
    us; we must save ourselves" (*Humanist Manifesto II,* p. 16).
    "Promises of immortal salvation or fear of external damnation
    are both illusory and harmful" (*Humanist Manifesto II,* p. 16).
    "As far as we know, the total personality is a function of a
    biological organism transacting in a social and cultural context.
    There is no credible evidence that life survives the death of the
    body" (*Humanist Manifesto II,* p. 17).

24. Page 17, *Humanist Manifesto II.*

25. Page 18, *Humanist Manifesto II.*

26. The contemporary pervasiveness of man-centered value systems is described by David Ehrenfeld, *The Arrogance of Humanism* (New York: Oxford University Press, 1978).

27. Page 18, *Humanist Manifesto II.*

28. Page 18, *Humanist Manifesto II.* This passage also states: "Short of harming others or compelling them to do likewise, individuals should be permitted to express their sexual proclivities and pursue their lifestyles as they desire" (*Humanist Manifesto II,* p. 18).

CHAPTER THREE

1. This observation was made by Shana Alexander in her television commentary on "Sixty Minutes," Columbia Broadcasting System, February 1978.

2. Alexander, *ibid.*

3. There is no doubt that "male chauvinism" is a distortion of true manhood and is one of the destructive extremes of what is commonly called "sexism," in modern-day parlance. We should certainly conclude that a "male chauvinist" attitude is a "sexist" attitude, with all the negative connotations that modern term usually carries. However, having said that, the reader is invited to reflect on the question: What is the opposite "sexist" extreme to male chauvinism? Does the word, "feminism" mean "feminine sexism"? Is it possible that "female chauvinsim" exists at the other extreme? These are some questions we will now explore. A legitimate Women's Movement was historically necessary to win the vote and other important social rights for women, to overcome the extremes and injustices of the "male chauvinist" attitude. The affirmation and recognition of normal femininity and the full personhood of women could be called a "normal feminism" or a normal, healthy sexism recognizing the equality of women in their social and political rights. But if there is a healthy, normal "feminism" that affirms the feminine, is there also the danger of an extreme form of "radical feminism" that is as "sexist" and destructive as the opposite extreme of "male chauvinism"? This is a question for the rest of this chapter.

4. Nancy Lehmann and Helen Sullinger, *The Document: Declaration of Feminism.* Minneapolis: Powderhorn Station, 1972, pp. 8, 9. This publication also states: "Liberated sexuality is freedom from oppressive stereotyping. The freedom to choose heterosexuality,

homosexuality, bi-sexuality, or a-sexuality but not to be bound by them."

5. *The Document: Declaration of Feminism,* pp. 11, 12.

6. *The Document: Declaration of Feminism* also states, under the subheading "On the Family": "The nuclear family must be replaced with a new form of family where individuals live and work together to help meet the needs of all people in the society" (p. 13). Under the next subheading of "On Children" this publication argues against the concept that a father and mother should care for their own children in a family setting: "We support parent controlled child care centers as a necessary step toward the feminist-socialist revolution, but our vision of the upbringing of children extends beyond them. With the destruction of the nuclear family must come a new way of looking at children. They must be seen as the responsibility of an *entire society* rather than individual parents. . . . This will teach them [children] the interdependence of people in a collective society" (p. 14).

7. Mary Samis, Tish Sommers, Marjorie Suelzie and Nan Wood (editors), *Revolution: Tomorrow Is NOW,* published by National Organization for Women, 1977. These proposals by the National Organization for Women are consistent with the radical feminists' goal to overthrow the ideal of a heterosexual marriage as the foundation for family care for children. The advocacy of free abortion, sterilization, and contraception for women is designed to "liberate" women from the responsibilities of motherhood as a unique female role.

8. *National Plan of Action Adopted at National Women's Conference, November 18-21, 1977, Houston, Texas.* Washington, D.C.: International Women's Year Commission, 1977.

9. This National Women's Conference was an activity of the "National Commission on International Women's Year," a commission authorized by an act of the United States Congress and funded by $5 million of federal tax money. According to the House of Representatives sponsor of the authorizing legislation, Congresswoman Bella Abzug, this "National Conference . . . will afford an opportunity for every kind of women, representing every viewpoint, in every State of this Nation to make a statement of her concern" (from the House debate by Congresswoman Abzug, December 1975). However, United States Senator Jesse Helms presented documentation to the U.S. Congress showing that a coalition of the National Organization for Women, the National Women's Political Caucus, the Lesbian Caucus, and other radical feminists deliberately

organized to eliminate fair representative participation in the various conferences of the "National Commission on International Women's Year" by women outside the militant feminist minority. In fact, the radical feminists circulated specific action plans designed to manipulate the outcome of voting sessions at the conferences to insure that only the radical feminist viewpoint would prevail. Their strategy included the philosophy, "Never give your enemy an even break." The "enemy" was defined as women who do not subscribe to the pro-abortion, pro-lesbian, anti-marriage positions of the radical feminists. See documentation by Senator Jesse Helms, "International Women's Year Activities: What Happened to Congressional Intent?" *Congressional Record,* July 1, 1977, volume 123, number 115, pages S11474-S11475.

10. This proposal is quoted here verbatim from the *National Plan of Action*; pp. 25 and 26:

REPRODUCTIVE FREEDOM

We support the U.S. Supreme Court decisions which guarantee reproductive freedom to women.

We urge all branches of Federal, State and local governments to give the highest priority to complying with these Supreme Court decisions and to making available all methods of family planning to women unable to take advantage of private facilities.

We oppose the exclusion of abortion or childbirth and pregnancy-related care from Federal, State or local funding of medical services or from privately financed medical services.

We urge organizations concerned with improving the status of women to monitor how government complies with these principles.

We oppose involuntary sterilization and urge strict compliance by all doctors, medical and family planning facilities with the Dept. of Health, Education & Welfare's minimum April 1974 regulations requiring that consent to sterilization be truly voluntary, informed and competent. Spousal consent should not be a requirement upon which sterilization procedures are contingent. If the patient does not speak English, appropriate staff must be found to explain the procedures and HEW regulations in the primary language of the patient.

Particular attention should be paid at all levels of government to providing confidential family-planning services for teenagers, education in responsible sexuality, and reform of laws discriminating against unwed parents and their children.

Programs in sex education should be provided in all schools, including elementary schools.

Federal, State and local governing bodies should take whatever steps are necessary to remove existing barriers to family planning services for all teenagers who request them.

Each school system should assist teenage parents with programs including child care arrangements that will encourage them to remain in school, provide educational and vocational training leading to economic independence, and teach prenatal health and parenting skills.

11. This proposal on "Sexual Preference" is quoted here verbatim from the *National Plan of Action*, page 27:

SEXUAL PREFERENCE

Congress, State, and local legislatures should enact legislation to eliminate discrimination on the basis of sexual and affectional preference in areas including, but not limited to, employment, housing, public accommodations, credit, public facilites, government funding, and the military.

State legislatures should reform their penal codes or repeal State laws that restrict private sexual behavior between consenting adults.

State legislatures should enact legislation that would prohibit consideration of sexual or affectional orientation as a factor in any judicial determination of child custody or visitation rights. Rather, child custody cases should be evaluated solely on the merits of which party is the better parent, without regard to that person's sexual and affectional orientation.

12. The verbatim proposal on "Child Care" from the *National Plan of Action* appears as follows on pages 7, 8:

CHILD CARE

The Federal government should assume a major role in directing and providing comprehensive, voluntary, flexible hour, bias-free, non-sexist, quality child care and developmental programs, including child care facilities for Federal employees, and should request and support adequate legislation and funding for these programs.

Federally funded child care and developmental programs should have low-cost, ability-to-pay fee schedules that make these services accessible to all who need them, regardless of income, and should provide for parent participation in their operation.

Legislation should make special provision for child care facilities for rural and migrant worker families.

Labor and management should be encouraged to negotiate child care programs in their collective bargaining agreements.

Education for parenthood programs should be improved and expanded by local and State school boards, with technical assistance and experimental programs provided by the Federal government.

City, county and/or State networks should be established to provide parents with hotline consumer information on child care, referrals, and follow-up evaluations of all listed care givers.

13. Quoted from the 1975 Ohio Task Force Report for the Implementation of the Equal Rights Amendment.

14. *National Plan of Action*, page 14.

15. Florida Network News, WRUF-AM, Gainesville, Florida, 2:30 p.m. broadcast on May 7, 1979.

16. Whereas the First Amendment to our United States Constitution may be properly interpreted as assuring that no single church be acknowledged or established as a state church, still the existence of God and the truth of his clear moral instruction stand as a consistent and clear supposition in all of our country's founding legal documents.

17. Reed Bell, M.D., speech to the Pensacola Kiwanis Club, Pensacola, Florida, February 8, 1978, page 9 of transcript. The author expresses appreciation to Dr. Bell for providing him original copies of many radical feminist publications that he and his wife, Nell, had collected after attending the November 18-20, 1977, National Women's Conference in Houston, Texas. My discussions with Dr. and Mrs. Bell served to sharpen my thinking about the deliberate anti-family tactics of the radical feminists. Reed and Nell, therefore, contributed substantially to my understanding of the political strategies of the radical feminists, and I gratefully acknowledge their contributions to my thinking in this chapter. Three additional manuscripts by Dr. Reed Bell that shaped my awareness of these issues are entitled:
    "Alienation—1978" written on April 10, 1978.
    "Viewpoint—Opposed: The ERA—The National Plan of Action," 1978.
    "Personal Report on Attending the National Women's Conference," 1977. Dr. Bell is the Director of Pediatric Services, Pensacola Educational Program and Chief of Pediatrics at Sacred Heart Hospital in Pensacola, Florida.

18. Reed Bell, "Personal Report on Attending the National Women's Conference," 1977, unpublished manuscript, page 6.

CHAPTER FOUR

1. Arndt and Gingrich suggest that this passage has been "textually damaged" (*A Greek-English Lexicon*, p. 865). In any event, they admit it is not an easy one to translate (p. 297). The question is, who is the subject of the verb "to long for" or "to desire"? If it is God, then the verse says, "He [God] yearns jealously over the spirit which he has made to dwell in us" (RSV). If it is not God, then "the spirit" is the subject, and the NEB translation is preferred. If it is the latter, and I think it is, then the "Scripture" that James says is speaking here is the entire creation account of Genesis. It is speaking of the powerful spirit of man which God has activated to fulfill the divine mandate to subdue the earth. The question raised in the context would be answered by noting that this restless spirit, when left unchecked by humility, is given to friendship with the world and causes untold conflict. It becomes a sworn enemy of God.

2. Harold Lindsell has discussed this problem in his book, *The Battle for the Bible* (Grand Rapids: Zondervan), 1976, pp. 117-121.

3. It was sad recently to hear an old friend espouse this newly-arrived-at position that came as a result of her commitment to "biblical feminism."

4. This is supported by White (*Expositors Greek Testament*, 4:107), Alford (*Greek Testament*, 3:317), Lock (*I.C.C.*, p. 31) and many others.

5. Many translations prefer to render the prepositional phrase adverbally—"quietly" (so read Berkeley, NASB, Moffat, Phillips, Goodspeed, and NEB).

6. On this word, see Moulton and Milligan, *Vocabulary*, p. 91, Robertson, *Word Pictures,* vol. IV, p. 570, and also Dibelius and Conzelmann, *Pastoral Epistles* (Hermeneia), p. 47.

7. This was so from the earliest times of the church. Tertullian in the second century (*On Baptism*, ch. 1) refutes an early heretic "with her venomous doctrine" by saying she "had no right to teach *even sound doctrine.*" (See also *On the Veiling of Virgins*, ch. IX; and Cyprian, *Treatise 46*).

8. This was a popular interpretation of the more classical commentators such as Ellicot and others.

9. Moulton and Milligan, in *Vocabulary* (p. 628), while rejecting this view, cite Ramsay's intriguing suggestion that the abstract form of the noun ("childbearing," *Teknogonia*) may refer in 1 Timothy 2 to

"motherhood" or "the power of maternal instinct." C.F.D. Moule (*Idiom Book*, p. 56), suggests it may mean, "just possibly," that the woman will be "brought safely through childbirth." Though plausible in its simplicity, the implied theology could be disconcerting if fully developed.

10. The word "image" (*Tzelem*) appears seventeen times in the Old Testament. A revealing use of the word appears in Genesis 5:3 where Adam bears a son in his own "image." To be in God's image is to be "like" him, to be able to respond to him. The uniqueness of man in Genesis 1 is that he is given moral obligations and preeminence over Creation. It cannot be denied that human sexuality is involved with being in God's "image." This is so, not only from the "male and female" emphasis of Genesis 1:27, but also from the word's appearance in other places (cf. Ezek. 16:17).

11. In Genesis 1:2, where the Spirit is said to be "moving over the face of the deep," the Hebrew word (*Merahepheth*) suggests the brooding flight of a mother bird guarding the nest (cf. Keil and Deilitzsch, *Pentateuch*, 1:49).

12. Glory is the visible expression of essence. The "Shekinah glory" of the Old Testament meant that God was with his people. When the Jewish distaste for blatant uses of the name of Jehovah became too great, common words were inserted to ease the tension. The Targums give evidence of this practice. In 1 Samuel 4:7, the simple statement "God has entered camp" was changed to "The Ark of God has entered camp." Isaiah said "I saw the Lord" (Isa. 6:1). The rabbis changed this to "I saw the glory of the Lord." These circumlocutions were common in the first century. "Glory" was the most common substitution. Thus we realize John's intention in the light of this practice when he said, "We beheld his glory" (John 1:14)— Jesus is God.

CHAPTER FIVE

1. Such is the understanding of many excellent commentators. Robertson and Plummer (I.C.C. *1 Corinthians* p. 320) note that "*psalmos*" appears only in Luke and Paul. St. John Parry (Cambridge Greek Testament, *1 Corinthians* p. 208) calls this a "psalm of his *own composition.*" G. G. Findlay (*Expositor's Greek Test.*, vol. 2, p. 907) says that, "Psalm indicates a larger reference than to the singing of the Old Testament Psalms; it included the improvised psalms. . . ." Findlay acknowledges that it may have included "an Old Testament Psalm Christianly interpreted," but it was probably "an original song" (p. 912). Grosheide (N.I.C. *1 Corinthians* p. 335) makes the assertion that these are psalms of

private composition owing to the unique use of the verb "to have," which is "to have on the basis of a special working of the Holy Spirit."

CHAPTER SIX

1. The humanistic world view clashes with the very structure of the universe. There are certain inextricable relationships between moral action and physical consequences. Illegitimate, immoral pleasure-seeking carries some automatic individual and social penalties. Sexual promiscuity yields the current epidemic of venereal disease. Tobacco smoking yields an incidence of lung cancer. Alcohol abuse results in health damage for the individual and automobile deaths for society. Indulgence in sadomasochistic pornography appears to lead to sexual perversion in the individual and in cases of rape for society (see Feshbach, Seymour & Malamuth, Neal. Sex and Aggression: Proving the Link. *Psychology Today,* November, 1978, pp. 111-117, 122; and Malamuth, Neal, Feshbach, Seymour & Jaffee, Yoram. Sexual Arousal and Aggression: Recent Experiments and Theoretical Issues. *Journal of Social Issues,* 33 (2), 1977). Homosexual behavior results in higher incidence of venereal disease for individuals and in broken families for society. These are illustrations of how the moral standards derived from the theistic world view could just as easily be derived simply from a serious study of nature itself (see also Rom. 1:18-27).

2. As cited by Dr. Amitai Etzioni, "Can We Do Without a Traditional Family?" Paper presented at the symposium on the family, Family— Our Responsibility, Sacred Heart Children's Hospital, April 4, 1979.

3. *Ibid.*

4. *Ibid.*

5. *Ibid.*

6. Note the selfish individual autonomy encouraged by the *Humanist Manifesto II,* as discussed in chapter two.

7. Etzioni, 1979, *ibid.*

8. Compare this modern attitude of glorified infidelity to the circumstance spoken of in Malachi 2:13-17, for an interesting parallel. The lack of wisdom in promoting marital unfaithfulness is seen in the joke section of *Family Weekly* (February 4, 1979, p. 21) in a contribution from David O. Flynn:

The professor was explaining the meaning of poetic justice to his class. "A good example," he said, "might be the philandering husband who meets his wife on a blind date."

9. Four types of venereal disease (syphilis, gonorrhea, Herpes Genitalis, and nongonococcal urethritis) are of particular significance due to their frequent occurrence in the industrialized nations of the world, although many other forms of venereal disease are also widespread (such as lymphogranuloma, venereum, cytomegalovirus, trichomoniasis, chancroid, and granuloma inguinale).

10. According to numerous standard reports of the United States Center for Disease Control, Atlanta Georgia.

11. Who are the people that contract venereal disease? Is it true that only irresponsible social deviants fall victim to this epidemic? Research studies have found that persons with VD tend to have a higher potential for impulsive behavior and extraversion than what is regarded as the norm (Gravitz, M. A., "Personality Correlates of Venereal Disease Experience," *Journal of the American Society of Psychosomatic Dentistry and Medicine,* 1973, 20 (1) 20-23. Hart, G., "Psychological Aspects of Venereal Disease in a War Environment," *Social Science and Medicine,* 1973, 7, 455-467). VD rates are highest among prostitutes, those who are fifteen to twenty-four years of age, military personnel, migrant groups, and homosexuals. Research confirms that homosexually active people have a much higher rate of VD than do heterosexuals. Incidence ranges from 10 percent to 77 percent. Male homosexuals tend to be among the most sexually promiscuous of individuals, engaging in frequent sexual relationships with many different partners—a large number of whom are such casual encounters that the partners never even learn each other's name. Many clinics are now reporting that 60 percent to 90 percent of male cases of syphilis are found in acknowledged homosexuals. Because of the many bisexuals (those who have promiscuous relationships with members of both sexes) abounding in our society today, a frightening reality has developed in that homosexuals have become a major contributor to the VD epidemic among promiscuous heterosexuals.

The stereotyped conviction that only an obvious counter-culture "type" gets VD is dangerously misleading. Many people have mistakenly believed that if they have sexual relations outside of marriage with a "clean-cut" partner they are "safe" from catching VD. Unfortunately, it is impossible to tell, either by dress or life style, who is and who isn't contaminated by VD. The simple fact is that so many people today are disregarding God's clear instruction to reserve sexual relations for a monogamous commitment sealed by the marriage vows, that it is virtually impossible to make a "good guess" as to who may or may not have VD.

See also these related articles: (1) "Doctoring VD Stereotypes," *Human Behavior*, January 1979, 8 (1) 26, 27. (2) Sgroi, Suzanne. "Kids with Clap: Gonorrhea as an Indicator of Child Sexual Assault," *Victimology: An International Journal*, 1977, 2 (2), 251-267. (3) Brayon, S. K., "Venereal Disease and the Teenager," *Journal of Clinical Child Psychology*, 1974, 3 (2), 30.

12. Our modern VD epidemic is a direct result of this current assault on marriage. One way to prove this is to look at the research studies which have compared the personalities of people with VD to the personalities of healthy people. Are these people any different than everyone else? On the one hand, studies have found that many individuals who get VD have scored significantly higher on personality test profiles associated with aggression, hostility, disregard for social standards, cynicism, exhibitionist trends, inability to learn from experience, emotional shallowness in sexual relations, impulsiveness, excitability, and overactivity (Gravitz, 1973). A research study by Dr. William Yarber at Purdue University and Dr. Robert Kaplan of Ohio State University found that males with VD were somewhat more serious and trusting than males without VD. However, females with or without VD reported the same level of moralistic reasoning. Similarly, males with VD reported themselves just as conservative as males without VD. A person's alleged moral values may not indicate whether or not he or she is in revolt against marriage. But actions will.

    We must conclude then, that some types of people, such as homosexuals or impulsive people, may be more likely to get VD, but anyone of any personality type could catch VD if he had sexual relations with a carrier of the disease. It is not possible, in general, to describe the type of person who revolts against the value of marriage. Apparently, the only commonality among these individuals is their sexual behavior outside of marriage which is often evidenced by their contracting venereal disease.

13. Drakeford and Hamm, 1973, pp. 28, 29.

14. Cline, Victor B., "An Assessment of Behavior Norms Modeled in Current Motion Picture Screen Plays," unpublished paper cited by J. W. Drakeford & J. Hamm, *Pornography: The Sexual Mirage* (Nashville: Thomas Nelson, 1973), pp. 59-62, 180.

15. Cline, 1973, *ibid.*

16. There appears to be a rapidly increasing preoccupation with sadomasochism in pornography. "But similar images have been creeping into advertising, fashion photography and the popular culture" (Feshbach & Melamuth, 1979, p. 111). Dr. Neal Melamuth, a U.C.L.A. psychologist, conducted a content analysis of five years of pictures and cartoons in *Playboy* and *Penthouse* and found that

the amount of sexual violence in those magazines has increased each year.

Psychological laboratory research at U.C.L.A. has found that the trail of aggression in books, magazines, and films can raise individuals' level of sexual arousal. On the other side of the coin, the research also found that materials that are sexually exciting can stimulate aggressive behavior.

Discussing their research on sadomasochistic pornography, U.C.L.A. psychologists, Drs. Seymour Feshbach and Neal Malamuth, emphasized:

For one of the most troubling results of our research suggests that men that view such material tend to be more stimulated by the idea of rape and less sympathetic to the victims (p. 111).

In discussing the results of their experiments on the influence of pornographic films on subjects' behavior, Drs. Feshbach and Malamuth discussed their findings in this way:

By showing the erotic film, we communicated the unspoken message that says, in effect, "Taboo behavior like sex is O.K. Feel free or partially free to lower the barriers." Evidently the barriers against aggressive behavior fell, too. We propose that sexual arousal is not a stimulus for aggression, but that a reduction in sexual inhibition will generalize to aggressive behavior where there are common taboos affecting sex and aggression (p. 114).

These experiments indicate, therefore, that pornography may not only lower the viewer's inhibitions against performing the sexual acts depicted, but may also generally lower other inhibitions, including urges to perform violent or aggressive acts.

In another psychological experiment, Drs. Feshbach and Malamuth studied the reactions of young men and women to erotic book passages describing rape. The experimenters varied the passages presented to the young men and women so that some of the passages described the victim as being in pain while other passages described the woman as finally giving in and enjoying the sexual act. These researchers found that for some of the men,

. . . . The fantasy of a woman becoming sexually excited as a result of a sexual assault reversed any inhibitions that might have been mobilized by the pain cues and by the coercive nature of the act. This finding is particularly worrisome if, as writers such as Susan Brownmiller have emphasized, the typical rape story in pornographic books and magazines portrays the woman as sexually aroused during the act (Feshbach & Malamuth, 1978, p. 114).

Drs. Feshbach and Malamuth point out that rape differs from sadism and masochism in which pain itself is the source of sexual gratification and in which the partners' involvement is usually voluntary. They then summarize another experiment that they conducted which found that men's exposure to sadomasochistic pornography influences their attitudes toward rape. After reading a sadomasochistic story, the male tended to be more sexually aroused in response to an account of a rape than other men who have read a nonviolent erotic story. In discussing the men's reactions to the rape stories, these researchers pointed out,

> . . . *The inhibitions that are ordinarily a response to pain cues (in the rape story) were somehow altered because of exposure to sadomasochistic material. Consistent with this interpretation was our finding that for these males, the greater their judgment of the victim's pain, the greater their sexual excitement. In contrast, for the males who had read the nonviolent version, the greater their perception of the victim's pain, the lower their sexual response. We see, then, how one exposure to violence in pornography can significantly influence erotic reactions to the portrayal of rape (Feshbach & Malamuth, 1978, p. 116).*

The influence of violent sexual pornography was suggested again when these experimenters asked the male subjects whether they would "behave as this man (the rapist) did under the same circumstances if it would be assured that you would not be caught and punished." Fifty-one percent of the men responded that they might carry out the rape if they were assured that they would not be caught.

These research psychologists concluded,

> . . . *The depiction of violence in erotica and pornography could be harmful (p. 117). The erotic presentation sometimes even approximates a how-to-do-it instructional film. Further, the juxtaposition of violence with sexual excitement and satisfaction provides an unusual opportunity for conditioning of violent responses to erotic stimuli. The message that pain and humiliation can be "fun" encourages the relaxation of inhibitions against rape (Feshbach & Malamuth, 1978, p. 117).*

Unfortunately, the use of violent sexual stimuli is not restricted to the materials in pornographic bookstores. A recent fashion layout in *Vogue* magazine, for example, featured a picture of a man brutally slapping an attractive woman.

CHAPTER SEVEN

1. *The Document: Declaration of Feminism*, p. 11.

2. To describe the traditional view of the motherhood role as it developed in the history of Western culture does not necessarily

imply that this traditional ideal was implemented by the vast majority of the population in most earlier eras. In fact, historians have found that working class women have not concentrated much attention on children in any period of history which has been studied. They were too busy working, as it turns out. The leisured class also shirked its responsibilities by "farming" their children out to working class nurses who, again, neglected their charges. As a consequence, what we are describing as the traditional role of motherhood was an ideal actually followed by only a small section of the population, and it served only as the implemented, general social ideal between 1780 and 1960, particularly in England. Consequently, the traditional ideal of devoted motherhood as we describe in this chapter can be traced back to earlier history in terms of its origin. The "traditional" view of the rights and responsibilities of motherhood as we describe it here should be considered desirable, not because it may or may not have predominated in particular past historical eras, but because of its appeal to moral conscience and because it can be one workable model for integrating the teachings of Judeo-Christian Scriptures to family life.

3. Although the use of various means of contraception is as old as the human race, it is a relatively modern phenomenon, within Western civilization at least, to view a completely childless home as a thing to be desired, and to use contraception as a means to such an end appears to be without historical parallel in our culture.

4. Hare-Mustin, Rachael T. & Broderick, Patricia C., "The Motherhood Inventory: A Questionnaire for Studying Attitudes Toward Motherhood," paper presented at the annual meeting of the American Psychological Association, Toronto, August, 1978.

5. Hare-Mustin, R. T., "A Feminist Approach to Family Therapy," *Family Process*, 1978, 17, 181-194. McBride, A. B., *"The Growth and Development of Mothers"* (New York: Harper and Row, 1973). Rich, A., *Of Woman Born* (New York: W. W. Norton, 1976). Rollin, B., "Motherhood: Who Needs It?" *Look*, September 22, 1970.

6. The January 1979 issue of *Money* magazine (vol. 8, no. 1) carried a special series of articles on "The Two-Paycheck Life"—referring to the fact that two spouses now hold employment outside the home in nearly 50 percent of American households, compared to 25 percent in 1950. The articles in this issue were entitled, "A Subtle Revolution" (by Edward E. Scharff), "Getting a Handle on the Urge to Splurge" (by Joseph S. Coyle), "Keeping a Working Marriage Working" (by Maryls Harris), "Making Money Without Making Waves," (by Jeremy Main), and "They've Grown Accustomed to Their Pay" (by Suzanne Seixas).

7. Associated Press, Washington. Survey: One in four pregnancies aborted. *Gainesville Sun*, April 30, 1979, page 12C. Religious News Service, New York. "Abortions World-wide," *The Christian Courier*, April 1979, p. 1.
8. See Ralph Smith (editor), *The Subtle Revolution: Women at Work* (Washington, D.C.: Urban Institute, 1979).
   Bernard, J. *The Future of Motherhood* (New York: Dial Press, 1974).
   Blumentahl, S. L. *The Retreat from Motherhood* (New Rochelle, New York: Arlington House, 1975).
   Bronfenbrenner, Urie, "Who Cares for America's Children?" In Victor Vaughan and T. Berry Brazelton (eds.), *The Family: Can It Be Saved?* (Chicago, 1976).
   Krause, C. A. *Grandmothers, Mothers and Daughters.* Survey by the American Jewish Committee's Institute on Pluralism and Group Identity, as reported in *Behavior Today*, July 31, 1978, 3-5.
   Lidz, T. , "The Effects of Children on Marriage," in S. Rosenbaum and I. Alger (eds.), *The Marriage Relationship: Psychoanalytic Prospectives* (New York: Basic Books, 1968).
   Lott, B. E., "Who Wants Children?" Some relationships among attitudes toward children, parents, and the liberation of women. *American Psychologist*, 1973, 28, 573-582.
   Minturn, L., and Lambert, W. W., *Mother of Six Cultures, Antecedents of Childrearing* (New York: Wiley, 1964).
   Russo, N., "The Motherhood Mandate," *Journal of Social Issues,* 1976, 32, 143-153.
   Sawchuck, Steven, "Family—A Problem." Invited paper at the Symposium on the Family presented at the meeting of Family—Our Responsibility, Sacred Heart Children's Hospital, Pensacola, Florida, April 4, 1979.

9. This statistic has its limitations in that it does not include live in domestic help and other groups difficult to tabulate. Nevertheless, such factors should not significantly alter our perception that there has been a major increase in the number of women working outside the home in the last 100 years.

10. As quoted by the Associated Press, *Gainesville Sun*, No. 81, September 15, 1979, page 1A.

11. Associated Press, *ibid.,* page 12A.

12. Harris, Marlys, "Keeping a Working Marriage Working," *Money,* 1979, 8 (1) 44-48.

13. These statistics are taken from the report, "The Status of Children, Youth and Families 1979," published by the United States Depart-

ment of Health and Human Services, Office of Human Development Services, Administration for Children, Youth and Families, Research, Demonstration and Evaluation Division, 1980.

14. Most children placed in various forms of child-care arrangements are not in group care, such as nursery schools or day-care centers. According to the 1975 statistics collected by the federal government, 49.7 percent of children were cared for by relatives (including 22.5 percent cared for in the child's home and 27.2 percent cared for in others' homes). Of these, 37.5 percent of the children were cared for by nonrelatives (including 20.9 percent in the child's home and 16.6 percent in other homes). Only 9.4 percent of the children were cared for in group care, including 5.8 percent in nursery schools and 3.6 percent in day-care centers. And 3.4 percent of the children were cared for in other ways. (Source: "The Status of Children, Youth and Families 1979," published by the United States Department of Health and Human Services, 1980.)

These same government statistics report that the population of United States children under five years of age was:
17,163,000 in 1970,
15,351,000 in 1978.
Although the fertility rate is expected to continue to decline, the absolute number of preschool-aged children is projected to increase between 1980 and 1990 because the post-World War II boom babies are in childbearing stage. The projected United States population of children under five years of age is therefore:
16,000,000 in 1980,
20,000,000 in 1990,
15,000,000 in 2000.
Now, putting all these figures together to get the complete picture at the end of the 1980s, we would make the following estimates, based upon the assumption that present trends will continue: By 1990, there will be 20 million children under the age of five. Since at least 50 percent of them will have mothers in the work force, they will need some kind of child care. If the 1975 pattern of child-care arrangements continues, this means that in 1990 there will be:
4.9 million children cared for by relatives
3.7 million children cared for in family day-care homes or in other homes
1.0 million children enrolled in child-care centers
0.4 million children cared for elsewhere.
The estimate of one million children enrolled in child-care centers in 1990 is the most conservative estimate and does not take into account the possibility that day-care centers may increase in numbers and in popularity.

15. "If we can generalize at all, we can say that all children at all ages need stability, continuity, and predictability in their human partner-

ships for the fullest realization of their potentials for love, for trust, for learning and self-worth. The human family . . . was invented for this purpose and while fallible at times, it normally provides the conditions for the fulfillment of these needs." Selma Fraiberg, *Every Child's Birthright: In Defense of Mothering* (New York: Basic Books, 1977), pp. 80, 81.

16. Carol A. Falender and Albert Mehrabian, "The Effects of Day Care on Young Children: An Environmental Psychology Approach," *The Journal of Psychology*, 1979, 101, 241, 255.

17. Selma Fraiberg, *Every Child's Birthright: In Defense of Mothering* (New York: Basic Books, 1977).

18. In reviewing the effects of day care for three-to-six-year-olds, Dr. Fraiberg concludes: "When preschool education is the family's only objective in bringing a child to a preschool program, the half day at nursery school is best adapted to the child's own needs. But when the primary consideration is *substitute care for a working mother employed full time*, the 9- to 10-hour-a-day group program can strain the child's tolerance to its limits. . . . As the 'consumer advocate' . . . it appears to me and others in the field of early child development that an 8- to 10-hour-day group care program for 3- to 6-year-olds does not serve the educational needs of small children, and the professional staff even under the most favorable circumstances find that they do not serve as 'mother substitutes' or 'teachers' beyond the half-day tolerance of most preschool children" (Fraiberg, 1977, pp. 86, 87).

19. Even in some child-care centers where there are favorable adult-to-child ratios, the children can experience adverse emotional effects. One research study of the effects of child care on children found substantial levels of fear of a stranger following the mother's departure, even though the ratio of adults to children was approximately one to three. H. Ricciuti, "Fear and the Development of Social Attachments," in M. Lewis & L. A. Rosenblum, editors, *The Origins of Fear* (New York: Wiley, 1974). In this study, the child-care facilities had a large turnover of adults in the setting, and little consistency in the caregiver-child relationship.

   Another study reported the assessment of the effects of four private, traditional, and unstructured nursery school programs (M. C. Blehar, "Anxious Attachment and Defensive Reactions Associated with Day Care," *Child Development*, 1974, 45, 683-692). In this study, the adult-to-child ratios ranged from one to six, to one to eight for the two- and three-year-old groups. This is an unusually favorable adult-child ratio for children this age, because most child-care programs have much higher ratios. However, the study found the day-care setting to be detrimental to the children's welfare, leading to "anxious attachment" between mother and child.

Some other studies have not found these particular negative effects of some other child-care programs. This apparent conflict in findings is discussed by Carol A. Falender and Albert Mehrabian in the previously cited theoretical review, "The Effects of Day Care on Young Children: An Environmental Psychology Approach," 1979.

20. Dr. Selma Fraiberg has reviewed the research evidence from many studies that lead to this conclusion: "The human capacity to love and to make enduring partnerships in love is formed in infancy, the embryonic period of development" (p. xi). She defines "mothering" as "the nurturing of the human potential of every baby to love, to trust, and to bind himself to human partnerships in a lifetime of love" (p. xi). In the latter half of the twentieth century in America, we are witnessing increasing numbers of children who have been deprived of a mother or mother substitute, and Dr. Fraiberg traces how these children suffer a diminished capacity to commit themselves to love as they grow up. Her book chronicles ". . . the devaluation of parental nurturing and commitment to babies in our society which may affect the quality and stability of the child's human attachments in ways that cannot yet be predicted" (p. xi and xii).

21. Solveig Eggerz, "What Child-Care Advocates Won't Tell You," *Human Events,* May 20, 1978, page 421.

22. Lewis, Claude. "The Family—How Relevant?" Invited paper at the Symposium on the Family presented at the meeting of Family—Our Responsibility, Sacred Heart Children's Hospital, Pensacola, Florida, April 4, 1979.

23. These sayings are among many collected by Albrecht Oepke in his excellent article on *"gunē"* in *Kittel (Theological Dictionary,* 1:776-789).

24. Namely: Prisca, Mary, Junias, Tryphena, Julia, and Nereus' sister.

25. A word borrowed, oddly enough, from Greek astrology (Arndt and Gingrich, *Lexicon,* p. 560). Appearing only here in the New Testament, it connotes a rule that is a strong influence on human life.

CHAPTER EIGHT

1. This case is reported in the scientific literature by G. A. Rekers and O. I. Lovaas, "Behavioral Treatment of Deviant Sex-role Behaviors in a Male Child," *Journal of Applied Behavior Analysis,* 1974, 7,

173-190. This article is also reprinted as chapter 25 in C. M. Franks and G. T. Wilson (editors), *Annual Review of Behavior Therapy and Practice* (New York: Brunner/Mazel, 1975). It is also reprinted as chapter 38 in G. R. Patterson, I. M. Marks, J. D. Mazarazzo, R. A. Myers, G. E. Schwartz, and H. H. Strupp (editors), *Behavior Change 1974: An Aldine Annual on Psychotherapy, Counseling and Behavior Modification* (Chicago: Aldine, 1975). This boy, with related cases, was first noted in an abstract published by G. A. Rekers and O. I. Lovaas, Experimental analysis of cross-sex behavior in male children, *Research Relating to Children*, 1971, 28, 68.

2. My clinical research has been funded by a National Science Foundation graduate fellowship (1970-1972) at the University of California at Los Angeles, a postdoctoral fellowship grant (1972-1973) at Harvard University from the Foundations' Fund for Research in Psychiatry, and United States Public Health Service research grants (1973-1980) from the National Institute of Mental Health (grant numbers MH21803, MH28240, and MH29945), the latter at the Logos Research Institute, Inc.

3. This conclusion is substantiated in the research I cite and report in the following academic articles on this topic:
    Rekers, G. A. "*A Priori* Values and Research on Homosexuality, *American Psychologist*, 1978, 33, 510-512.
    Rekers, G. A., "Atypical Gender Development and Psychosocial Adjustment," *Journal of Applied Behavior Analysis*, 1977, 10, 559-571.
    Rekers, G. A. "Pathological sex-role Development in Boys: Behavioral Treatment and Assessment" (doctoral dissertation, University of California, Los Angeles, 1972). *Dissertation Abstracts International*, 1972, 33, 3321B. (University Microfilms No. 72, 73, 978).
    Rekers, G. A., "Psychosexual and Gender Problems," chapter 11 in E. J. Mash & L. G. Terdal (eds.), *Behavioral Assessment of Childhood Disorders* (New York: Guilford Press, 1981).
    Rekers, G. A., Bentler, P. M., Rosen, A. C., & Lovaas, O. I., "Child Gender Disturbances: A Clinical Rationale for Intervention," *Psychotherapy: Theory, Research, and Practice,* 1977, 14, 2-11.
    Rekers, G. A., & Milner, G. C., "Early Detection of Sexual Identity Disorders," *Medical Aspects of Human Sexuality*, 1981, in press.
    Rekers, G. A., & Milner, G. C., "Sexual Identity Disorders in Childhood and Adolescence," *Journal of the Florida Medical Association*, 1978, 65, 962-964.
    Rekers, G. A., Rosen, A. C., Lovaas, O. I., & Bentler, P. M., "Sex-role Stereotypy and Professional Intervention for Childhood

Gender Disturbances," *Professional Psychology*, 1978, 9, 127-136.

Rosen, A. C., Rekers, G. A., & Bentler, P. M., "Ethical Issues in the Treatment of Children," *Journal of Social Issues,* 1978, 34 (2), 122-136. Reprinted in *Eta Evolutiva*, 1979 (an Italian scientific review).

Rosen, A. C., Rekers, G. A., & Friar, L. R., "Theoretical and Diagnostic Issues in Child Gender Disturbances," *The Journal of Sex Research*, 1977, 13 (2), 89-103.

Mead, S. L., & Rekers, G. A., "The Role of the Father in Normal Psychosexual Development," *Psychological Reports*, 1979, 45, 923-931.

4. I have published a number of academic book chapters and journal articles on my clinical research in this area, which the interested reader could locate in library study:

Rekers, G. A., "Assessment and Treatment of Childhood Gender Problems," chapter 7 in B. B. Lahey and A. E., Kazdin (eds.), *Advances in Clinical Child Psychology* (Vol. 1) (New York: Plenum, 1977).

Rekers, G. A., "Childhood Identity Disorders," *Medical Aspects of Human Sexuality*, 1981, 15, in press.

Rekers, G. A., "Sexual Problems: Behavior Modification," chapter 17 in B. B. Wolman (ed.), *Handbook of Treatment of Mental Disorders in Childhood and Adolescence* (Englewood Cliffs, New Jersey: Prentice-Hall, 1978).

Rekers, G. A., "Sex-role Behavior Change: Intrasubject Studies of Boyhood Gender Disturbance," *The Journal of Psychology*, 1979, 103, 255-269.

Rekers, G. A., "Stimulus Control over Sex-typed Play in Cross-gender Identified Boys," *Journal of Experimental Child Psychology*, 1975, 20, 136-148.

Rekers, G. A., Lovaas, O. I., & Low, B. P., "The Behavioral Treatment of a Transsexual Preadolescent Boy," *Journal of Abnormal Child Psychology,* 1974, 2, 99-116.

Rekers, G. A., & Mead, S., "Early Intervention for Female Sexual Identity Disturbance: Self-monitoring of Play Behavior," *Journal of Abnormal Child Psychology*, 1979, 7 (4), 405-423.

Rekers, G. A., & Mead, S., "Female Sex-role Deviance: Early Identification and Developmental Intervention," *Journal of Clinical Child Psychology*, 1980, 8, 199-203.

Rekers, G. A., & Milner, G. C., "How to Diagnose and Manage Childhood Sexual Disorders," *Behavioral Medicine*, 1979, 6 (4), 18-21.

Rekers, G. A., & Varni, J. W., "Self-monitoring and Self-reinforcement Processes in a Pre-transsexual Boy," *Behavior Research and Therapy*, 1977, 15, 177-180.

Rekers, G. A., & Varni, J. W., "Self-regulation of Gender-role

Behaviors: A Case Study," *Journal of Behavior Therapy and Experimental Psychiatry,* 1977, 8, 427-432.

Rekers, G. A., Willis, T. J., Yates, C. E., Rosen, A. C., & Low, B. P., "Assessment of Childhood Gender Behavior Change," *Journal of Child Psychology and Psychiatry,* 1977, 18, 53-65.

Rekers, G. A., Yates, C. E., Willis, T. J., Rosen, A. C., & Taubman, M., "Childhood Gender Identity Change: Operant Control Over Sex-typed Play and Mannerisms," *Journal of Behavior Therapy and Experimental Psychiatry,* 1976, 7, 51-57.

I have also written a number of closely related articles that provide research support and rationale for the treatment procedures that are presented in the articles above:

Bentler, P. M., Rekers, G. A., & Rosen, A. C., "Congruence of Childhood Sex-role Identity and Behavior Disturbances," *Child: Care, Health and Development,* 1979, 5 (4), 267-284.

Ferguson, L. N., & Rekers, G. A., "Non-aversive Intervention for Public Childhood Masturbation," *The Journal of Sex Research,* 1979, 15 (3), 312-223.

Rekers, G. A., Amaro-Plotkin, H., & Low, B. P., "Sex-typed Mannerisms in Normal Boys and Girls as a Function of Sex and Age," *Child Development,* 1977, 48, 275-278.

Rekers, G. A., Crandall, B. F., Rosen, A. C., & Bentler, P. M., "Genetic and Physical Studies of Male Children with Psychological Gender Disturbances," *Psychological Medicine,* 1979, 9, 373-375.

Rekers, G. A., & Mead, S., "Human Sex Differences in Carrying Behaviors: A Replication and Extension," *Perceptual and Motor Skills,* 1979, 48, 625, 626.

Rekers, G. A., & Rudy, J. P., "Differentiation of Childhood Body Gestures," *Perceptual and Motor Skills,* 1978, 46, 839-845.

Rekers, G. A., Sanders, J. A., & Strauss, C. C., "Developmental Differentiation of Adolescent Body Gestures," *Journal of Genetic Psychology,* 1981, 138 (1), 123-131.

Rekers, G. A., & Yates, C. E., "Sex-typed Play in Feminoid Boys vs. Normal Boys and Girls," *Journal of Abnormal Child Psychology,* 1976, 4, 1-8.

Rosen, A. C., & Rekers, G. A., "Toward a Taxonomic Framework for Variables of Sex and Gender," *Genetic Psychology Monographs,* 1980, 102, 191-218.

5. For example, see the following articles written in specific objection to my research designed to prevent homosexuality, transsexualism, and transvestism:

Morin, Stephen J., & Schultz, Stephen J., "The Gay Movement and the Rights of Children," *Journal of Social Issues,* 1978, 34 (2), 137-148.

Nordyke, N. S., Baer, D. M., Etzel, B. C., and LeBlanc, J. M., "The Implications of the Stereotyping and Modification of Sex-role," *Journal of Applied Behavior Analysis,* 1977, 10, 553-558.

Winkler, R. C., "What Types of Sex-Role Behavior Should
    Behavior Modifiers Promote?" *Journal of Applied Behavior
    Analysis*, 1977, 10, 549-552.

6. For example, see 1 Samuel 4:9.

7. Marion Howard, "The Young Parent Family," chapter 22 in Victor
    C. Vaughan and T. Berry Brazelton (editors), *The Family: Can It
    Be Saved?* (Chicago: Year Book Medical Publishers, 1976),
    pp. 239-255.

8. See the review by Urie Bronfenbrenner, "Who cares for America's
    children?" Chapter 1 in Victor Vaughan and T. Berry Brazelton
    (editors), *The Family: Can It Be Saved?* (Chicago: Yearbook
    Publishers, 1976), as well as other chapters in the book on that same
    topic.

9. See Victor Vaughan and T. Berry Brazelton, 1976.

10. See Victor Vaughan and T. Berry Brazelton, 1976. Also, compare
    these figures with those cited in our chapter seven. See also the book
    by Ralph Smith (editor), *The Subtle Revolution: Women at Work*
    (Washington, D.C.: Urban Institute, 1979).
       Unfortunately for child development, it is the younger mothers,
    particularly the ones under twenty-five years of age, who constitute
    the highest percentages of employment outside of the home
    (Bronfenbrenner, 1976). Although some young mothers seek jobs
    outside the home because of the low earnings of their husband's
    early career, it turns out that the most rapid increase in working
    mothers occurs in the middle and high income families. Dr.
    Bronfenbrenner has pointed out that the mothers from middle
    income families in the 1970s were entering the work force at a much
    higher rate than did married women from low income families in the
    early 1960s.
       But by far the highest rates of employment of mothers are in the
    group of single-parent homes. About two-thirds of the homes with
    incomes under $4000 contain only one parent. Single parenthood is
    the most common for young families in the low income brackets.
    Overall, it is the single-parent mother who is in the most severely
    strained financial situation. There are more than a million-and-a-half
    single mothers with children who survive with a median income of
    only $2800. This represents one-third of all the female-headed
    families with children under six years.
       In all, the black families in American society are the most vulner-
    able. In fact, in the late 1970s more than half of black children were
    born out of wedlock. This is a sharp increase from 1965 when 26
    percent were born out of wedlock. In contrast, white children born
    out of wedlock were 4 percent in 1965 and 7.7 percent in 1976. Only
    six years ago 30 percent of all black children lived in single-parent

families headed by their mother, while in the late 1970s, the statistic moved up to 40 percent of black children, as compared to 12 percent of white children. This means that increasing numbers of American children are being raised without the father in the home.

11. In addition to the book by Vaughan and Brazelton, 1976, the reader is referred to reviews of these and related research findings in:
   Yankelovich, Skelly & White, Inc., *The General Mills American Family Report—1976-1977: Raising Children in a Changing Society* (Minneapolis: General Mills, 1977).
   The October 1976 issue of *The Family Coordinator* (vol. 25, no. 4) contains twenty-two academic review articles on social science research on the topic of "Fatherhood."

EPILOGUE

1. Leon Trotsky, *Stalin: An Appraisal of the Man and His Influence* (New York: Stein & Day), 1967 (p. xv).

2. Robert E. Speer, *The Finality of Jesus Christ* (Grand Rapids: Zondervan), 1968, p. 14.

TOPICAL INDEX